TIME TO L

TIME TO DECLARE

30 Years in the Customs Front Line

John Clarke

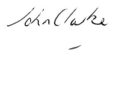

ASHWATER
PRESS

Designed and published for John Clarke by
Ashwater Press
68 Tranmere Road, Whitton, Twickenham, Middlesex, TW2 7JB

www.ashwaterpress.co.uk

Printed by The Dorset Press, Dorchester, England

ISBN 978-0-9927119-6-2

Contents

Background

With the rise of budget airlines, international air travel has never been easier or more affordable. Consequently most of us have returned to a UK airport and had to run the gauntlet of passing through the customs controls. The popularity of programmes such as 'Nothing to Declare' is evidence of our fascination with the customs officer's job. Most people have inquisitive natures and the customs detection role is the dream job for bringing out the inner Nosey Parker. I spent over 37 years in the job having joined HM Customs and Excise from school in 1978 and served over 30 years in the front line at Gatwick Airport. This book is a personal account that tells you about many of the smugglers we caught and sheds some light on why we stop the people we do. There are also many anecdotes from my time at Gatwick, some of which date back to an age that wasn't quite so politically correct.

Introduction

It was a Friday night in 1987 and a young Nigerian man was in a hotel near the airport in Lagos. If you'd taken him back a bit in time he would never have envisaged being there, especially for the purpose he now found himself engaged in. However, his father had become seriously ill and, with hungry mouths to feed at home and no welfare state to fall back on, he had fallen prey to temptation. A so-called friend with links to ruthless drug traffickers knew of his vulnerability and had put him in touch with a gang member specialising in the recruitment of couriers. The young man was told he'd be paid £500 if he'd take some packages of drugs to London, an absolute fortune to him but a fraction of their worth to the traffickers once sold on the streets in the UK. He was told that if he hid the packages inside his body it would be impossible for customs officers to find them, so there was no risk of him being caught. This wasn't the only lie he was told; he certainly wasn't told that if the packages burst inside him and got into his bloodstream he might very well die. Unsurprisingly the gang had no concern for him as a person; they only wanted him to act as a mule for their precious cargo.

At the time he was in the hotel secreting the packages he'd been given, a young customs officer in London was contemplating the weekend ahead. He'd joined the department from school somewhat by accident and was still early in his career as a detection officer at Gatwick Airport. He was rapidly finding his feet, though, and was looking forward to an early shift the next day when he would have the chance to test his newly-acquired skills on a number of interesting and high-risk flights. As he set his alarm that night to ensure he'd be at the airport in time for the early-arrival plane from Lagos, the young Nigerian had just finished stuffing his packages and was being taken to the airport with the new passport and air ticket his paymasters had supplied. They had also armed him with a cover story to help him get through immigration and strict instructions on where he should go to deliver the packages.

With a following wind he would have sailed through the border controls on his arrival in London on that Saturday morning. However, when he was called forward to present his passport it was his misfortune that the young customs officer, who had just come on duty, had decided from seeing his nervous demeanour in the queue that his might be a story worth listening to. It was a decision that proved to be right as a very short while later the Nigerian was being arrested on suspicion of importing a controlled drug. The meeting of the young Nigerian and the young Londoner had been something of a fateful coincidence, albeit a happy one for the latter. It was one of many for that customs officer, who just so happens to be me. I hope you'll enjoy some of the other stories I have to tell.

Chapter 1

EARLY DAYS

I was born at home in Streatham in south-west London in August 1962. My dad, Don, was a butcher by trade and, prior to having my sister Debbie and me, my mum, Jean, was a switchboard operator for the GPO (General Post Office), the forerunner of what we now know as BT (British Telecom).

We were just a typical family growing up in 60s Britain; I was too young to know that they were allegedly swinging at the time. We moved out to leafy North Cheam in 1968 when there was a

A young me contemplating a career at Craven Cottage rather than Gatwick Airport.

threat to build a ring road through our back garden, and I spent the rest of my formative years in the London borough of Sutton which to be fair is not as leafy as I'd like to recall.

In 1973 I took a test known as the eleven plus which I didn't think of as significant at the time. This exam has long since been discarded into the dustbin of history but my passing of it meant I was offered a place at grammar school. Hence in September of that year I started at Sutton Manor High School for Boys whilst my sister and nearly all my mates went to the co-educational comprehensive down the road.

This probably benefitted me in terms of my education and ability to pass my GCEs but left me sadly lacking in the experience of dealing with the fairer sex. Consequently whilst I was being taught chemistry, physics and religious studies, in amongst other 'fascinating' subjects, my mates all seemed to be acquiring girlfriends. The fact that I was benefitting from a quality education seemed to me to be scant consolation for my pitiful lack of success with the ladies.

The summer of 1978 was significant for two reasons: the World Cup and my O-Levels. England's failure to qualify for that summer's finals was another episode of the country's never ending failure to repeat the triumph of 1966, a success I'm sadly just too young to remember.

I'm also a lifelong Fulham fan, so it's fair to say failure and I aren't exactly strangers. However, England's absence from Argentina 1978 did probably help me manage to pass eight of my exams. As it was I did a negligible amount of revision with the World Cup on, but had the Three Lions been there I'd most likely have done none at all.

Eight passes were very important to me as will become clear. Most of my peers at Sutton Manor were staying on for A-Levels and were on the path to university. On the other hand yours truly never particularly enjoyed school and was well aware that my mates at the comprehensive were leaving school at 16. Therefore I felt that the need to earn beer vouchers of my own outweighed any desire to extend my illustrious stay in education.

As a result in March 1978, after a little research in the school careers library, I started applying for jobs. The trouble was I had absolutely no clue what I wanted to do. The only real career I fancied was in journalism but once I realised this would entail a minimum of two years at college my enthusiasm waned. My parents thought I'd be bright enough to blag some sort of office job; my abysmal efforts in the woodwork class proved (if any proof were necessary) that I would struggle with anything practical. I don't know if the bar was set lower in those days but within a short time I'd had interviews and received job offers from the Co-op Bank, Department of Trade and Industry, NatWest Bank and the GLC (Greater London Council). I accepted the first offer I got (from the Co-op Bank), giving me the insurance of a job while I went for other interviews.

The last interview I attended was for a clerical officer post in HM Customs and Excise. The interview took place at Custom House, just past Billingsgate Market on the north side of London Bridge. I remember my train was delayed that morning so I had to run from London Bridge station to make the interview on time. I was 15 at the time so jogging was indeed possible in those days, although I can't say I've made a habit of it since. As a result a rather sweaty and nervous teenager went into an interview that was far from an unqualified success. My interrogator spent most of the time expressing astonishment that I was leaving a good grammar school education and tried to persuade me that A-Levels and university was the route for me. I left the interview a little discouraged, but my escort out of the building told me what a good job Customs was. He also gave me a copy of the latest edition of Portcullis, the Customs staff newspaper. He said that it would give me a flavour of what the department did. His kindness did far more to sell Customs as a career to me than my actual interviewer did.

Bearing in mind how the interview went I was somewhat astonished to be offered a post as clerical officer a week or so later. The letter informed me that the offer was dependent on me passing five O-Levels that coming summer, so the main decision now was which job to pick out of those I'd been offered. My inherent laziness helped with the whittling down process. Both bank jobs indicated that I would need to study for an Institute of Bankers exam if I wanted to progress. More study was anathema to me so the banking industry dodged a bullet there. It's a pity that some thirty years later they (or more particularly the British taxpayer) weren't so lucky.

This left a choice between the Department of Trade, Customs and the GLC. The DoT seemed a bit too stuffy for my liking so it came down to the GLC or Customs. Fortunately I chose Customs as it just seemed to have more potential. This time it was my turn to dodge a bullet as within a few years 'Red' Ken Livingstone, by now the leader of the GLC, had pissed Margaret Thatcher off so much that she abolished it. For such a supposed exponent of democracy it seemed rather harsh but as Arthur Scargill and the miners found out you didn't mess with the Iron Lady.

Therefore I spent the post exam summer of 1978 sweating that my revision-light approach had paid off and that I'd get the five passes needed for the job I wanted. Eight O-Levels meant I'd made it with a bit to spare. Perhaps in hindsight I had revised too much… I informed Customs of the glad tidings and in due course received a letter asking me to report for duty at the Custom House on 11th September 1978.

Chapter 2

REPORTING FOR DUTY

The rest of the summer of 1978 went by in a blur. I actually left school a month before my 16th birthday as my mum got my headmaster's permission to leave at the end of June since I wouldn't be coming back for A-Levels. I did a few odd jobs to earn enough money to buy a pair of Doc Martens. I wasn't exactly a 'bovver boy' but rather wanted them as a fashion statement! I'm not sure what I was trying to say though; they certainly didn't increase my success with girls.

I continued with my paper round and intended to try to keep it going until Christmas. My Christmas box (tips from customers) had made me £30 in 1977, a small fortune in those days. I didn't like the thought of my replacement getting that sort of money for three months' work when I'd done most of the hard graft. Hence, when Monday 11th September came around, my first day in the employ of HM Customs and Excise was my second job of the day. This state of affairs lasted only as long as the receipt of my first salary, when I realised £30 wasn't such a fortune and that getting up before 6am to do a paper round wasn't great preparation for a day at work.

I reported for duty at the same venue I'd had my interview, Custom House in Lower Thames Street, along with eleven other fresh-faced and nervous individuals. We then underwent some basic induction training that gave us an overview of the department and what our role as clerical officers would entail. We also discovered the delights of the Custom House bar every lunchtime, where not only were prices subsidised but also the staff were too polite to ask if we were over 18. The downside to this stroke of good fortune was the afternoons when some of the more mundane aspects of our training left a few of us struggling to stay awake. We were all told that we would be given posts somewhere in headquarters. HQ London, as it was more commonly known, was a 'collection' in its own right; Customs and Excise was split into collections, a historic term used for the different areas of the country.

HQ London was located in various office buildings dotted around the city, with each housing a particular section. Towards the end of our induction we were all handed bits of paper telling us where we were being appointed. Mine said 'IB' on it which meant absolutely nothing to me. My trainer told me it stood for Investigation Branch and that I should report to their staff section at Harmsworth House in Bouverie Street, where I would find out more. In hindsight this piece of paper was the reason that I ended up pursuing a career in Customs.

On completion of my induction I duly turned up at Harmsworth House where I was told the IB was now known as the ID (Investigation Division). I was being appointed to the Valuation Team whose leader was Stuart Wesley, SIO (senior investigation officer). Beneath him were some HEOs (higher executive officers), an EO (executive officer) and yours truly at CO (clerical officer). My role was to provide clerical support to this fine band whose role was to investigate fraud committed by companies seeking to evade paying customs duty. It was called the Valuation Team because a common way of evading duty was by undervaluing imported goods. Another common fraud was misdescription. All the different duty rates were contained in a publication called the Tariff, a weighty tome some 99 chapters long. By misdescribing an item it was possible to attract a lower rate of duty. I remember one company was done for evading

HM CUSTOMS AND EXCISE
Investigation Division
14 New Fetter Lane London EC4A 1PA

Telephone 01-353 6500   Telex 23426 CEIDLN G

sak

Mr J D Clarke
CO
Investigation Division
London

Your reference

Our reference

Date 6 November 1979

Dear Mr Clarke

CLERICAL OFFICER APPOINTMENT

I am pleased to inform you that your twelve months
probationary period of service has been satisfactorily
completed and your appointment as Clerical Officer is
duly confirmed.

Please accept my congratulations and may I wish
you every success in your future career.

Yours sincerely

C L Shakeshaft
Principal (Administration)

I'm in. The department had their chance – and missed it!

duty on pistachio nuts, there being different rates for raw and roasted nuts. It wasn't the most elaborate fraud as they merely tippexed out the letters after the 'r' on the supporting invoices and replaced them with the letters that got the lower duty rate.

We were a busy team who had plenty of companies under investigation. My line manager, Will Robinson, EO, was a great bloke and I immediately felt comfortable on the team whose ethos was work hard, play hard. One of the HEOs was a wonderful chap called Neil Perrin whose path I would cross later in my career at Gatwick Airport, where he was ultimately in charge as the assistant collector. He gave me some sage advice on my first day: never admit you can type (not an issue for me anyway) and always carry a pen and bit of paper around with you so you look busy. These tips have held me in good stead over my career; after all a certain amount of window dressing doesn't do any harm.

Over the next three years I had a whale of a time. Although the work itself was fairly routine, I got plenty of trips away with the boys, acquiring documentary evidence to support a case. I also saw at first hand how boring some of the other jobs in HQ were. I think that if I been posted anywhere other than the Investigation Division I would have looked for pastures new quite quickly. As it was, I loved the work and although as a CO I didn't go on any 'knocks' (the day when the team would walk into a firm unannounced to ensure an element of surprise and that documentary proof of fraud couldn't be destroyed) I felt a valued member of the team.

By 1981 I had enough confidence and experience to apply for promotion. I loved the ID but to be an EO in Investigation you had to be vetted. Fortunately this wasn't a process requiring the removal of any parts but it did involve a lengthy process quite separate from promotion. In any event I had seen up close the long hours that specialist investigators had to work. They were paid an allowance but they were expected to work a certain amount of overtime for it. In my experience most were so dedicated that they went far beyond what was required. It got the job done but it was often at the expense of family life and in many cases marriage. As a (still) single man I wanted the chance to find a partner before I ran the risk of losing one, so I knew that with regret I'd have to leave the ID.

Summer 1981 and my application resulted in an interview for the exalted position of executive officer. I can't remember much of what happened there but my blagging skills must have paid off as a short time later I was informed I was on the promotion list. I then had to choose a vacancy from those available. The fact that I took a post at Croydon VAT Office was far more a result of its proximity to my home in Sutton than any desire to be a taxman. My last day in the ID was the 6th November 1981, a date that was marked with (not for the only time in my stay there) a sherbet or two.

Chapter 3

THE DREADED TAXMAN

So, with promotion achieved I started the next stage of my career at Croydon VAT Office, which was housed within a huge office building close to East Croydon railway station. The town seemed to be full of these sort of skyscrapers which led to the wind whistling round in all directions. Consequently it always made me think of Chicago which was known as the 'windy city' and was also apparently Frank Sinatra's kind of town. I'm not sure that the old crooner ever thought of Croydon quite as fondly but it suited me down to the ground being an easy commute from Sutton.

I started life at Croydon as a VAT control officer which effectively meant I was visiting traders to check books and accounts to ensure their VAT returns were accurate. I still hadn't learned to drive so was relying on public transport to get to my appointments. This was fine for visits to leafy Selsdon and Sanderstead, but colleagues had told me that trips to New Addington weren't quite as inviting. There only seemed to be one road in and one road out and I was told that if you upset the wrong sort of trader on the New Addington estate then a quick getaway could be imperative.

Fortunately my few trips there passed off without incident as did all my time on VAT Control. Being junior meant I was primarily visiting small businesses with small turnovers. Often they were sole traders who were only just over the threshold limits for the tax. Normally most kept their own books so I was visiting private dwellings where I was generally greeted with a sense of trepidation, probably similar to the sense of fear I had when I started doing visits on my own. Once I realised that they were more nervous than me I coped fine. I was always treated with the utmost courtesy and normally got a cup of tea and a biscuit for my troubles. In hindsight it must have been quite an ordeal having your books checked by the dreaded taxman, even if in my case it was only a pimply 19-year-old rather than a bowler-hatted stormtrooper.

After a couple of years on Control I was moved on to the Enforcement District which as the title suggests was a little more forceful. Enforcement meant the collection of debts and often meant visiting traders with the bailiff in tow in order to secure payment of their VAT. Lots of traders were used to this sort of brinkmanship, and to assist with their cash flow would only ever pay up when the bailiff was on the doorstep. However in some cases they genuinely couldn't pay and it was quite distressing to see businesses and people's hopes and dreams go under.

In general I was enjoying my time in VAT but temptation had been dangled in my direction. Several officers at Croydon had arrived on promotion from Gatwick Airport and they all told me how desperate they were to get back there. They all said how much more interesting the work was and more importantly how much more money they could make there in terms of shift pay and overtime. I was astonished that they had all taken pay cuts for being promoted, the difference between the two grades' salary not being as much as they'd been getting for working weekends and overtime. I was told that if you got to Gatwick on officer's pay you were doing very nicely indeed.

I discussed the idea with my boss and he encouraged me to put in for a transfer. He said that a move to Gatwick would be good for promotion prospects. I therefore applied and didn't have to wait long before I was posted to Gatwick to start there

To all to whom these Presents shall come Greeting.

We the Commissioners of Her Majesty's Customs and Excise

pursuant to the powers in that behalf vested in us **Do Hereby** appoint

JOHN DAVID CLARKE

....

to be an **officer** of Customs and Excise and to be employed on any Duty or Service which We may from time to time direct and approve with full power and authority to do and perform all such matters and things as are by any Act of Parliament in force relating to the Revenues of Customs or Excise or any other matter assigned to the Commissioners of Customs and Excise directed or authorised to be done and performed by an officer of Customs and Excise and to enforce all laws, regulations, penalties and forfeitures as directed by the Commissioners of Her Majesty's Customs and Excise in all which premises he is to proceed in such manner as the law directs hereby praying and requiring all and every Constable and member of Her Majesty's armed forces or coastguard and all others whom it may concern to be aiding and assisting to him in all things as becometh the said....JOHN DAVID CLARKE

....

to observe and obey all such orders instructions and directions as he hath received and shall from time to time receive from the said Commissioners and to hold the office to which he is hereby appointed during the pleasure of the said Commissioners.

In Witness hereof I the undersigned being one of the Commissioners of Her Majesty's Customs and Excise have hereunto set my Hand and Seal at King's Beam House, London, this...25th....day of....January...................19...82....

Officer's Commission

My officer's commission, issued after my promotion to Croydon VAT office.

as a collection officer in May 1985. Fortunately I had passed my driving test that February so was all set for airport life. On the downside, eight officers who remained at Croydon all got promoted later that year. The only people who missed out were those of us who put in for transfers. I think that when my boss said a transfer was good for promotion prospects he obviously didn't mean mine.

KD

HM CUSTOMS AND EXCISE
19-29 Woburn Place London WC1H 0JQ
Telex 266008 Cusex Ce Ldn
Telephone 01-632 239 9\25

Mr J.D. Clarke
Officer
Croydon LVO

Your reference

Our reference
85126/P
Date

25 April 1985

Dear Mr Clarke

I am pleased to inform you that the Board by their order EST/385/200/16 dated 22 April 1985 have approved your transfer to EO, Gatwick Collection Officers, London Airports Collection.

The transfer will be at Crown expense under the provisions of Establishment Instructions Part 3, on the understanding that a removal of home will not be necessary.

Will you please report on Monday 17 June 1985 to:

Mr J. Eastland
Senior Officer
Room 512
South Office Block
Gatwick Airport
Gatwick
W. Sussex   RH6 0LX   at 9 am.

(Access is by the domestic departures.)

Yours sincerely

Hilary Chambers

H. CHAMBERS
Officer Staff Section 2

My letter confirming my transfer to Gatwick Airport.

Chapter 4

CUTTING MY TEETH

Monday 20th May 1985 heralded the start of my career as a genuine customs officer. Although by that time I had spent seven years in the department I hadn't considered myself a customs man before then. My work in the Investigation Division involved the sort of clerical work that could be done in pretty much any office, while in my opinion the VAT job had more in common with the Inland Revenue.

On my first day I reported for duty to the fifth floor of an office building above what is now the south terminal of Gatwick Airport. It wasn't referred to as the south terminal in those days as it was the only terminal, the north terminal not opening until 1988. I was told that the first thing they needed to do was measure me up. Fortunately they meant for uniform rather than anything more final. Visions of a swift and brutal ending to my nascent career were therefore averted.

I was quickly assigned to a training course which I was told would be at the London Airports Collection training centre at Harmondsworth near Heathrow. For the next few weeks I did a daily commute from Sutton for a lot of classroom training and role plays. Although there was much to take in I found it both interesting and rewarding. On the course with me was another new Gatwick officer who has remained a good friend and colleague throughout my career. We would later work on the same team and play together for the Customs football side. Latterly 'Moaner', which was one of the more affectionate nicknames coined for him, would actually be my boss. Moaner has a somewhat mournful disposition and has been known to do more than his fair share of complaining. However I have to say he is a lovely bloke at heart who truly cares about the job.

It was therefore a stroke of fortune that on returning to Gatwick I was told I would be mentored together with Moaner. Our mentor was to be a chap called Steve Webb; 'Spider' was a kind mild-mannered individual and he was just the right character to help us put what we had learned in theory into practice. We started by observing him pull passengers and question and search them. Once we were confident enough he got us to do the interceptions ourselves although he did indicate which passengers he wanted us to stop. He started us off on what he thought would be fairly easy and compliant passengers so that we could practise our technique without too much stress.

At that time we were concentrating on what were commonly known as 'bucket and spade' flights which essentially comprised holidaying Brits returning from their annual trip abroad. In amongst the sombreros and toy donkeys, many holidaymakers would sneak in an extra bottle or carton or two, and it was on these sort of punters that Spider got us to cut our teeth. The allowance for booze and baccy was one litre of spirits and 200 fags or 250 grams of tobacco, rules that for non-EU flights still apply to this day. It wasn't therefore too difficult to find people with more than their allowance.

If we found passengers in excess they were dealt with in one of two ways. If the amount wasn't excessive they could be dealt with by way of a 'petty' seizure. I believe at the time the limit was £30 revenue. If the amount of tax involved was less than that, the goods were merely seized and restored for the revenue involved plus 10%. If the revenue was more than £30 the consequences were more serious. The passenger would be formally interviewed with a view to establishing a Section 170 offence. This referred to a section of the Customs and Excise Management Act that covered being knowingly concerned in the fraudulent evasion of duty. If we could prove that, then the punter would be subject to a fine of double the revenue involved. Even if we couldn't prove fraudulent intent, the fine would still be single revenue, and in both circumstances restoration of the seized goods cost even more.

In those days many revenue seizures were still being made. A lot of the older officers had grown up on them before drug smuggling really came to the fore. Not only that but prior to Margaret Thatcher abolishing them soon after she came to power, officers were actually paid seizure rewards. Thatcher's argument for removing them was that officers were being paid a wage to seize goods so why should they be paid a reward on top. It was a reasonable theory although it didn't really take the human nature of wanting to earn a bit more into account. Seizure rewards were self financing anyway as they only represented a small proportion of the revenue recovered, so for an administration that trumpeted the creation of wealth the decision seemed rather perverse.

In any event it wasn't long before I got my first 'job', the more common term for a seizure. It wasn't exactly earth-shattering stuff, just a 68-year-old Canadian visitor with three extra bottles. It was just a 'petty' but I still had to formally caution him and ask why he hadn't declared them. His answer was that the steward on the plane didn't explain to him what he needed to declare. This was the first of any number of excuses I was to hear as to why goods had not been properly declared, and to be fair it wasn't the worst. Although the gentleman may have thought the steward was to blame it was he who was relieved of £27 to get his bottles back.

My next job was off a Guernsey flight which was significant for two reasons. It was the only time I seized a bottle of Martini and it was the first time I heard the excuse 'My wife packed the case and I didn't know they was in there.' I was to hear many more variations on this theme over the years.

I was rapidly getting the hang of knocking off these small revenue jobs although the nerves did kick in when I caught a bloke coming back from Tenerife with a few extra bottles. It transpired he was a serving police officer so I was very concerned that I'd get the wording right when I cautioned him. What I hadn't accounted for was that he was in a far worse state having being caught breaking the law. When I asked why he hadn't declared them his reply was 'I can't say much to that.' He obviously couldn't bring himself to say 'It's a fair cop, guv.'

After a few weeks mentoring I was signed off as being a competent officer and was ready for my first posting. I'd been appointed as a collection officer which meant I was not assigned to a fixed post but instead would be covering different vacancies around the airport. It was an ideal way to start as it gave me the opportunity to experience many different roles as well as meet an awful lot of colleagues. To start with I was put on a baggage team in the terminal which was a continuation of what I'd been doing in my training. I was put on Alan Hayes's Yellow team which was a great place to start. Alan was a fantastic bloke whose only real fault was being a QPR supporter. He had a team full of characters, many of whom were vastly experienced. They taught me much about the job as well as how to assiduously use the downtime between flights.

On my first night shift with the team I was summoned to the rest room where I was offered what was known in the trade as a 'nobbler', which would be a glass of rum, brandy or whatever else was in the team locker. Officers returning from holidays abroad would declare a 'docking bottle' which would be constructively warehoused by the team on duty. They would then helpfully test the contents of the said bottle to destruction on their next run of nights.

Being new to the game I asked whether it was alright to imbibe whilst on duty only to be told it would be considered rather poor form if I didn't. It was my first introduction to a culture that probably got its traditions from the old Waterguard of Customs, so called because prior to air traffic most customs work centred on sea ports. Customs officers would routinely board vessels and would normally be offered a welcoming libation from the ship's captain. Many of my new colleagues had worked at ports and informed me that the main job of an assistant officer was to get his officer safely back off ship if they had over-availed themselves of the captain's hospitality.

Today it would be a disciplinary offence to drink alcohol on duty, but in those days the culture was completely different. People in all walks of life and professions would go to the pub in their lunch hour. In actual fact when I started at Gatwick there was even a bar at the airport staff canteen, although thankfully you were far more likely to see a customs officer drinking there than a pilot. In that sense drinking in the downtime between flights didn't seem so wrong. The odd officer over-indulged but I can say hand on heart that for most it never affected their ability to do the job when it mattered. I could probably even produce statistics to support this argument as in my early days at the airport more drugs seizures were made on nights than on any other shift. This was partly because we had an early morning arrival from Lagos which was an absolute goldmine for us.

Anyway, I thoroughly enjoyed my time on Yellow team even without a glass in my hand, and it was during my time with them that I had my first significant revenue seizure when I caught an Irish labourer on a Dublin flight with an extra 1,000 fags and ten bottles of vodka. It was a good job he was a labourer as his bags certainly took some lifting.

Chapter 5

MOVING ON

My next posting was to the Tarmac district which operated out of Concorde House adjacent to the terminal building. They were responsible for boarding all arriving planes to check that the in-flight bar boxes were sealed and also to rummage the plane for any hidden contraband. A common method of drug smugglers was to secrete packages within an aircraft before it departed, for instance behind a panel in the toilets. Airport staff at this end would retrieve the drugs and take them off the airport in a works vehicle or at the end of their shift.

Another common ploy was what is known as 'rip on/rip off'. This would involve airport staff at the place of departure 'ripping on' a rogue bag with a bogus baggage tag. This tag would be identified at this end by crooked loaders who would 'rip off' the bag and ensure it never got to the reclaim carousel. Again they would take it off the airport at any opportunity, normally in a work van purportedly going about its normal business. Hence Tarmac were also responsible for gate checks which involved searching any vehicle leaving the airfield. The trouble with this was as soon as a gate check was set up the bush telegraph sounded and any dodgy vehicle would leave by a different gate or wait until we'd gone. As you can see drug smugglers can be downright sneaky bastards who would invariably be one step ahead of the game. We did have some success with these rip off gangs though mainly thanks to a lot of hard undercover and surveillance work by our Investigation staff.

Another responsibility of the Tarmac district was crew clearance. Every arriving aircrew had to make a written declaration and hand it in as they left the airport and potentially subject themselves to being checked by Customs. This could have been good news for me as any number of glamorous hostesses would pass your gaze on a shift. However I was still pretty shy at the time and so felt rather intimidated in their midst. Some of the more experienced officers had no such qualms though and knew a lot of the regular flyers well. In fact one day I recall the senior officer digging one of the staff out for using a hostess's first name and being, as he put it, 'over familiar'. The officer's reply was succinct and to the point: 'It's a bit hard not to use their first name when the last time you saw them they had your cock in their mouth, sir.' It was pretty hard to respond to that, which was just as well as the riposte left his boss speechless.

As you can probably guess I enjoyed my brief sojourn on Tarmac. There were so many larger than life characters that every shift was fun and I was told lots of stories, most of which were no doubt true. The most notorious tale was the one referred to as the 'Gatwick option'.

Significant revenue seizures were punishable by way of a fine, but this was optional as one could elect to reject this and have the case heard by a magistrate instead. The infamous Gatwick option came about when a Tarmac senior officer took a shine to a hostess who had transgressed. Instead of going to court, the option allegedly offered was carried out in a locked room at the Gatwick Satellite and involved a form of corporal punishment rather than payment of a fine. Some say the world is now too politically correct and this may not be as shocking as some of the cases uncovered in the wake of the Jimmy Saville scandal. However, this sort of behaviour was a shocking abuse of power and had no place in any workplace let alone a law enforcement organisation such as ours.

My next job was covering at Biggin Hill for a few weeks. This is a small airfield in Kent that it was Gatwick's responsibility to administer. The officer on duty there was responsible for customs and immigration matters so I was given the briefest of courses on how to stamp a passport should the need arise. Little did I know then that eventually I would have to be fully trained as an immigration officer when the UK Border Agency came into being.

I was there during the winter months so it was far from hectic. I was told that it got much busier in summer and that quite often you'd see the rich and famous and especially the stars of Formula One arriving on their private jets. However, it was a pleasant enough environment to work in and as it wasn't my 'home station' I was picking up mileage and subsistence allowances to boot.

My next stop was the courier facility, which was a small shed on the perimeter road where all the parcels from the likes of DHL were cleared. Larger amounts of cargo were cleared at the freight sheds on the far side of the airport but the courier traffic was much lighter and easier to deal with. To be honest it was fairly boring there as you were never likely to find much more than personal use amounts of drugs in a packet or an envelope. I was already missing the cut and thrust of the baggage hall, so I was chuffed when I was told I had a permanent position on Dave Sawdon's Green team.

Chapter 6

A PERMANENT FIXTURE

It was February 1986 when I joined the Green baggage team which consisted of the senior officer, six officers (including yours truly) and three assistant officers. Baggage teams were responsible for pretty much anything involving passengers and their baggage. You therefore rotated your duties between the green and red channels and outward baggage which was commonly known as OB; cunning abbreviations were a way of Customs life. OB duties mainly consisted of stamping foreign visitors VAT forms, which necessitated checking that the goods they'd purchased on holiday were being exported and qualified for the tax to be refunded. It wasn't sexy but it was necessary work. Over my years at Gatwick many fraudulent claims were uncovered. In one particular case an organised crime group were claiming tax back on allegedly high value jewellery that was actually costume quality. The sums involved had cost the exchequer revenue running into millions.

Red channel duties were particularly busy back in 1986. In addition to the drink and tobacco allowances there was a limit to the amount of other goods you could bring in, which at that time was only £28. We had two early morning arrivals from Hong Kong every day and it was pretty impossible to have done any shopping there and spent under £28. Consequently the queue for passengers waiting to declare goods often stretched across the reclaim hall even when we had two or sometimes three tills open. Some passengers saw the length of the queue and would try to dart through the green channel, but we always had our eyes peeled for that.

Dishonesty wasn't restricted to the green, though, as we always had to be alert for partial or under declarations in the red. Although red channel work could be mundane, in respect of having to wait for people to come to you, the sport of spotting an 'underdec' was where the fun lay. We had a variety of techniques at our disposal.

In addition to the Hong Kong passengers we got a lot of people declaring carpets and leather jackets on return from Turkey, and we knew for a fact they would have two or sometimes three receipts for their goods. One would be higher (for insurance purposes), one would be lower (for Customs) and one would be for the actual price paid. Obviously punters would declare their goods at the lowest price and would happily proffer you the bent receipt. Lots of people weren't very sophisticated with their deception, though, and were a little shocked when we asked them to produce their wallets or purses, where lo and behold we found more receipts for the same item. We could have actually seized their goods, as an offence had been committed, but we normally settled for taking the correct amount of tax, with the satisfaction that their faces were as red as the channel they'd entered. You could also see the people in the queue behind quickly start to adjust which receipt to show you.

Some of the more determined fraudsters took more catching though, and this is where our supplies of bovine manure, otherwise known as bullshit, came in handy. In the case of Turkish carpets we knew that the more knots per square inch the rug had, the more intricate the work and the higher the value. We would therefore ask for the carpet that had been declared to be produced, at which point the red channel magnifying glass was brought into play. We would peer through the lens in the manner Sherlock Holmes would look at a piece of evidence and murmur our appreciation of the Turkish craftsman's work. A typical observation would say how fantastic their rug was and how we couldn't believe they'd got it for that price, and were they sure they hadn't paid more? It was a game of bluff which we often won when the real receipt emerged from the passenger's pocket.

Sometimes, though, determined travellers, who these days are probably playing online poker, would try to see the charade through. This is where we used our pièce de la résistance (the C104 form) which involved making a signed declaration as to the true value of the goods. Before we asked for the form to be completed we drew their attention to the paragraph that said making a false declaration could lead to fines and/or imprisonment and asked them to initial it to indicate they understood. Many a poker player would fold at that stage and so prove the old adage that you can't bullshit a bullshitter.

I do recall one passenger insisting the receipt he'd produced for his very expensive £500 carpet was genuine, and he signed the C104 to that effect. Call us cynics but we still thought he'd paid more for it than he was prepared to admit. We therefore detained it and took it to an expert in Horsham who told us that the piece was a load of old tut and wasn't worth more than £50. When we returned the item to the gentleman we didn't have the heart to tell him he'd been ripped off, and so took tax on the £500 he'd declared it at. After all, that's what he said he'd paid.

The best days on a baggage team were those where you were rostered to work in the green channel. This gave you more chance to put the skills you were acquiring into operation. It was good to observe the more experienced officers at work and they were happy to pass on their knowledge if you asked why they had stopped a particular person. You quickly learned what the higher risk flights were, and so you could hone down your selections from the more random stops you'd done in your training. At that stage I was moving on from bottles and cartons to better quality revenue seizures. A particular feather in the cap at the time was to detect a high value watch in the green channel. Rolex was a very popular make at the time and plenty of them were being smuggled in on the daily Hong Kong flights.

Many people thought that if they wore their new purchase under a long sleeve we would never find them. It therefore became a habit to ask passengers if they were wearing a watch and ask to see it. If the watch looked new it would lead us to further questions. Often we were told that the watch was old or it had been bought tax paid in the UK. If they thought that would lead us to say 'Thanks very much, on your way,' then they were sorely mistaken. I hesitate to say people are stupid but in my experience they are often naive.

My first Rolex seizure was on a gentleman's wrist and he gave me the usual spiel about having bought it in London 18 months ago. Unfortunately for him his Rolex came in a nice presentation box which he had helpfully left in his suitcase along with the warranty and the receipt from a jeweller's in Hong Kong from his trip. Further experience taught me that most people are very reluctant to throw away receipts, particularly those for high value items.

I would therefore start most searches on a Hong Kong flight looking through wallets and document folders. Once you'd found a receipt for a nice watch or piece of jewellery you knew it was worth your while escalating the rest of your examination. We also knew where the serial number on Rolex watches was hidden should someone insist they had bought the watch here. A phone call to Rolex with the serial number and they could tell you exactly where in the world the item had been retailed.

Over subsequent years the other goods allowance went up significantly; it currently (in 2019) stands at £390. As a result the amount of revenue detections started to dwindle, especially as we had to prioritise other more harmful commodities. Although this was fair enough, I look back with fondness at those days of copious revenue seizures. It was still smuggling and involved you identifying the dishonest from the honest passenger, skills that are very necessary whatever you are looking for.

Chapter 7

HAVING WHAT IT TAKES

A lthough I was making a good variety of seizures in my early days at Gatwick, my overriding ambition was to start detecting drugs. There were specialist officers, known as the baggage crews at the time, whose only task was to find prohibited drugs, and they naturally were making the majority of the airport's seizures. Typically they were very experienced officers who had 'done their time' and who'd proved their aptitude for catching drugs smugglers.

Baggage team officers found their fair share but as they had other responsibilities they didn't get as many opportunities to hit the good flights. Also the baggage crews could be a bit territorial. A lot of the time they worked at the disembarkation gates or in passport control where they would listen to the reasons a passenger might give to the immigration officer for their visit. If they got a whiff of a dodgy story they would 'bag' that punter and follow them until they'd picked up their case and then intercept them as they tried to exit customs. Consequently they didn't like anyone from the baggage teams wandering down to the immigration hall and getting in their way.

Often I'd be working in the reclaim hall and spot a 'decent bet' only to see a baggage crew officer following close behind. This meant the passenger was off limits, and woe betide anyone stopping someone whom another officer already had eyes on. This practice was known as stroking and was very much a taboo in the Customs game. I witnessed many arguments between officers where the stroker would plead innocence and claim they didn't realise a colleague had already 'bagged' a passenger. The strokee would seldom accept this excuse and instead would get quite cross. Indeed if the passenger turned out to have drugs the strokee could become apoplectic as they saw the kudos of a drugs detection and the overtime that went with it end in somebody else's lap. Healthy competition like this was seen as good by management, though.

Most staff were highly motivated to find drugs and I was no exception. Stuffers and swallowers were starting to arrive in numbers in the mid to late 1980s and we had to 'babysit' them on overtime. Babysitting was the term we used for guarding the prisoners whilst they slowly but surely produced the packages they'd secreted internally. It wasn't pleasant work but detainees often took many days to expel all the packages until they were clear. That meant there was plenty of overtime to be shared out. This gravy train provided great soothing balm for any internal divisions and helped pay a lot of mortgages at a time of soaring interest rates.

As a single bloke still living at home I wasn't so much motivated by the prospect of extra money but more by the need to prove myself to my peers. As I was still quite new I wasn't getting too much pressure from above to start finding drugs. It was just that I wanted to feel worthy of being in the company of colleagues who were regularly making drugs seizures and who I wanted to emulate.

I will go into the reasons we stop people in a little more depth later but often the key to making a detection is simply being in the right place at the right time. This was certainly true on 16th April 1986 when I was working at the front of the green channel (rather than being stuck in the red channel or OB), waiting for the Eastern Airlines flight from Miami to come through. I was aware that this flight had decent connections from the Caribbean and knew that seizures had been originating from there. As a result there were normally a lot of baggage crews in attendance, but on this particular day they didn't seem to be around. I therefore didn't have to stroke anyone as I saw a woman of about 30 approach customs with a trolley full of luggage. Once she'd made her way into the green nothing-to-declare channel I stopped her and immediately saw she had transfer tags on her bags which told me her journey had originated somewhere before Miami.

I asked to see her passport and ticket but my suspicions grew as she told me she'd thrown her ticket away and the alarm bells grew even louder when she said she had only visited America on her trip. It seemed to me she was trying to disguise the fact she'd been elsewhere. The deception couldn't last long. After all, I could see that her bag tag showed she'd had her bags transferred on to Gatwick from another flight into Miami and the stamp in her passport showed she'd been to the Cayman Islands. I asked her why she hadn't told me she'd been there but she was quite evasive and getting visibly more nervous. I therefore quickly started to examine her bags and immediately found a package wrapped in brown tape in her hand luggage, which she said contained books.

It didn't feel like books and the wrappings were consistent with the way many packages of cannabis were being concealed. I therefore slit the package open to reveal a herbal substance that was unmistakably cannabis. At this stage adrenalin was running through my body and I'm sure I was feeling equally as nervous as the woman in front of me. 'It's not books, is it?' I said to the woman. I've always had an uncanny gift for stating the bleeding obvious. 'No,' she admitted and quickly told me she had more packages in the rest of her luggage and that she'd been asked to bring the drugs by someone else. I managed to mumble out the arrest and caution and escorted the lady and her luggage to the cells in our accommodation.

Fortunately for me the woman was co-operative and compliant and made a full confession. She had been laid off from work and had agreed to courier back some drugs to help her pay off her debts. She ultimately pleaded guilty to smuggling 12 kilos of cannabis at court, which spared me the ordeal of giving evidence but didn't spare her from a significant custodial sentence. Guidelines for drug offences at that time were quite severe even for class B substances.

Having a drugs seizure under my belt was quite a relief and also gave me a greater sense of satisfaction than any other seizure I'd made. Like anybody in a new job it takes time to build up confidence and competence and getting that first drugs detection was the biggest boost I could have had. I was starting to really enjoy the work and began believing that I might have what it takes to be a customs officer.

Chapter 8

A DAY IN COURT

With my first drugs job under my belt I was settling in well on Green team and thoroughly enjoying my first permanent posting at the airport. In June I got another small cannabis seizure, thanks to what we called an 'immigration turn out'. If an immigration officer wasn't completely satisfied that a passenger was a bona fide visitor to the UK, they would detain them for further examination. This might involve talking to the alleged sponsor of the visit or making other background checks. It would certainly mean that the punter would be brought to customs to have their baggage checked. In those days immigration didn't have the powers or training to search baggage so we would do the 'turn out' on their behalf, hence the phrase. Immigration would be interested in documentation which might suggest the passenger was really coming here to work or settle; this would give them grounds to refuse entry. However, if immigration thought the visit might be suspect it could also be an indication that the true purpose might be to smuggle drugs. Therefore we were only too happy to assist with a baggage search as it might mean gold dust for us.

In this case it was a 24-year-old singer from Jamaica who was allegedly here to sign business papers. His nervous demeanour led me to carry out a search of person, and in the sole of each shoe I found a package which the gentleman told me contained ganja (cannabis). He later admitted his guilt in interview where I resisted the temptation to ask if he was a sole singer. Although there wasn't a huge amount, he was still charged and dealt with by the magistrates on the following day, when he got a short custodial sentence and was recommended for deportation. That pair of shoes probably turned out to be the most expensive he's ever had.

My next drugs seizure was from another immigration turn out. This time it was a Brazilian who'd travelled via Madrid and was ostensibly here for a friend's wedding. In a jeans pocket in his bag I found a small wrap of herbal substance which he admitted was pot. I then found some more in a plastic film container which he said was marijuana given to him on the plane. He didn't specify by who but I can't imagine it was part of the in-flight meal. In certain circumstances, essentially where it was a class B drug and a very small amount, we could offer a similar option to revenue offences. This would be payment of a fine instead of going to court, and this is what happened on this occasion. Therefore I was a year past my basic training and still hadn't had to give evidence in court. We had done some role plays and attended a couple of hearings but I was told nothing really prepared you for giving evidence and more particularly being cross-examined.

This was soon to change and it was on a case that wasn't even my own detection. Glenn 'Sleasy' Parisi was a young assistant officer who had started at the airport soon after me. Glenn became a good friend so I would have to say his nickname was more due to rhyme than his behaviour. Nicknames were a way of life at Gatwick. I have always been known as Nobby – in fact many colleagues claim not to know what my actual first name is. Incidentally Nobby is commonly associated with the surname Clarke rather than anything relating to size or girth. My dad was also known as Nobby and when I first went to the pub with him his mates called me 'Little Nob' in order to distinguish us; and before anyone asks, they hadn't been looking.

Anyway, to get back to the story, Glenn can't have long finished his training when he made a brilliant find on a Nigerian man he had stopped on the early morning Lagos flight. He had an electric iron in his bag which is a fairly unusual thing to carry and warranted Glenn's close attention. The upshot was that he found over 50 grams of heroin hidden under the base plate. A further 130 grams was found in the soles and heels of a pair of shoes. As Glenn was assistant officer grade he needed an officer to assist him and carry out the interview. Unfortunately he drew the short straw and got me. Interviews at the time were carried out using a C&E 1227 form which was where you wrote down the questions and answers. The cutting edge of technology hadn't quite reached us then and the use of cassette tapes to record interviews was still a couple of years away. Handwriting questions and answers was obviously not ideal as, unlike a tape, what was recorded could be open to dispute.

Things went smoothly enough on the day but no admissions of guilt were made, so it was no surprise to find that our friend had pleaded not guilty at his first hearing. It meant Glenn and I would both have to give evidence for the first time at his crown court trial. We were obviously very nervous when we attended court at Chichester.

Witnesses can't discuss the case once they've given evidence, so I couldn't speak to Glenn once he emerged from giving his evidence looking ashen faced. It was my turn next and although it wasn't too bad being led through my evidence by prosecuting counsel, nothing had really prepared me for the ordeal I was to face under cross-examination. The defence counsel accused us of planting the drugs and subjecting his client to the most vile racist abuse during his time in custody. Although the accusations were outlandish, my training had told me not to react but to calmly refute them. This I did although I have to say it was a most unpleasant experience.

As I said, handwritten interviews were not ideal but we always offered them to the client to read and then sign to say if it was an accurate account. This is exactly what our friend had done. Not only that but his solicitor had been present throughout and had also signed the record. It all made his accusations look rather preposterous, and consequently the jury took just over an hour to deliver a unanimous guilty verdict. Glenn and I were mightily relieved and were even happier when defence counsel came over to apologise and compliment us on the way we had given our evidence. He could see we were young but was surprised when we told him it had been our first time in the witness box. I told him there were no hard feelings; after all he was only doing his job.

Over the years I've given evidence many times, and although I was always nervous it did gradually become easier. Until our internal procedures changed, if it was your detection it also meant you were the case officer. This meant you put the whole file together for our solicitors office and attended court for the entire trial. It meant you liaised closely with the prosecuting barrister, which was both an interesting and rewarding experience. They had often only read the file on their way to court so would be eager to pick your brains for more insight into the case. Although most were from a completely different background, I found all of the ones I dealt with to be polite and interesting company. Not only that but on most days they insisted on buying your lunch.

The main drawback of court was that it could be very time consuming. Most cases were put on a 'warned list' which meant they could start on any day within a two-week time frame. Life had to go on hold until a case was called, and even then things could be delayed by legal argument or technical requests. Much time was spent hanging around before you got to give your evidence. In fact, when the department introduced a court awareness training course, I suggested that 90% of it was spent outside the classroom waiting to go in.

Chapter 9

STUFFERS AND SWALLOWERS

As you can imagine, smugglers will go to pretty much any lengths to hide their contraband. We had been shown pictures of elaborate concealments on our training course but there was no better teaching aid than physically seeing how drugs were hidden. Consequently, if you were on duty when a drugs job went down, officers queued up to take a look, especially if it involved a method not seen before. Tried and tested techniques included hiding the gear inside foodstuffs such as hollowed out yams. The mud and dirt you'd expect to see on the outside was smeared over where the incision had been made to hide the stuff, so there was really no substitute for cutting a thing open. Later, when we had use of an x-ray machine, we didn't have to hack things apart so often, but to be fair it was the only way you could be 100% sure there were no drugs inside an item.

Other common methods I saw in my early days at the airport were concealments inside wooden carvings or hollowed out books. Tinned foodstuff was popular and often the smugglers could commercially seal the cans, so again the only way to check was to get the tin opener out. We had a tool room with enough drills, chisels, hammers and suchlike to make a carpenter green with envy. With this array nothing was beyond our gimlet-eyed perusal. False-bottomed hard-sided suitcases were all the rage as well. A slightly smaller suitcase was glued inside a bigger one with a healthy portion of drugs shoved in the space between. Again drilling and hacking an item apart were the favoured methods of examination. Of course, many innocent travellers had items damaged in the process. They were directed to your friendly senior officer who would try and appease them and hand out a leaflet about compensation.

I might be giving the impression that we were gratuitously hacking people's prized possessions to pieces, but this wasn't the case. We only extended our examinations to the lengths considered necessary and it was inevitable that occasionally there would be collateral damage. If we'd exhausted our search of baggage but still had our suspicions then we would seek authority to carry out a search of person. Body belts containing drugs or packages taped around the legs were a common method of concealment and these could be found on a 'rub down' search. However, sometimes smaller packages were secreted in underwear so often only a strip search would do.

As we got more and more successful at finding drugs concealed in these ways smuggling gangs took things up another notch with the advent of the internal concealment. We referred to the couriers they used as stuffers and swallowers, another example of our imaginative thinking.

People often asked me what would possess a person to risk their life by swallowing packages of drugs that, if they split inside them, would kill them. I can't speak so much for now but back then there was certainly a lot of naivety about the danger, particularly in the poorer countries we were catching most smugglers from. The vast majority of our jobs were on flights from Nigeria, Ghana and Jamaica where, if a person was down on their luck, there was no welfare state to fall back on. Consequently many of the couriers we caught were desperate just to get money to feed their families, a fact gangs would prey on ruthlessly. Commonly they would offer the courier about £1,000-£2,000 in cash which would be a small fortune to them but what was just a small fraction of what the drugs were worth once they'd been cut and sold on here. Further they would say nothing of the risk to health, and convince them that, if they hid the drugs inside them, then Customs would have no chance of detecting them.

It's true at the time that there weren't many technological aids such as body scan machines to fall back on, but we were far from weaponless in our methodology. Port Health doctors were happy to be called out by us if a suspect was willing to be examined. They received a tidy fee from the department for their trouble and in one year one particularly busy medic had his transatlantic holiday paid for by Her Majesty. There were a couple of doctors we tried not to use as much, being as they were often on the medicine themselves. There was one famous or should I say infamous occasion where our MD put a glove on only to insert an ungloved digit into the passenger's rectum. Stuffed packages were readily detectable by the doctors we used though, and they could often tell from abdominal examinations if a person was likely to have swallowed.

By the late 80s we also had the 'EMIT' machine which was able to test a suspect's urine for drugs. Although sometimes a positive result was explained by previous use rather than internal concealment, the machine was another great help in detecting swallowers. Our best asset though was patience. Often a passenger would refuse to co-operate. We couldn't compel them to give a urine sample or be examined by a doctor so it often became a waiting game. By and large the innocent passenger would comply and try to prove their innocence at the earliest opportunity. A lack of co-operation generally meant there was something to hide and as we were on overtime our patience was endless. The law of nature was bound to win and it wasn't long before you would hear the familiar thud of packages hitting the pan. Never was the phrase 'where there's muck there's brass' more apt.

Sifting packages was not a particularly pleasant task. We now have space-age-looking, hermetically sealed units in which business takes place, but back then they sat on a loo you'd more commonly see at a music festival. Produce ended in a plastic bag which you'd physically have to sift in a vegetable colander. You did gown and mask up but it was still a hands-on experience you could have lived without. The hardest thing to get used to was being in the room whilst your suspect took a dump. We obviously had to be there to ensure chain of evidence (no pun intended). There was normally quite an awkward silence whilst business was taken care of although I wasn't adverse to a bit of small talk to ease the passage. All of these experiences held me in good stead for nappy duties when I had children of my own. After what I'd seen, my own kids' nappies were quite literally a piece of piss.

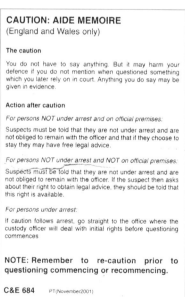

CAUTION: AIDE MEMOIRE
(England and Wales only)

The caution

You do not have to say anything. But it may harm your defence if you do not mention when questioned something which you later rely on in court. Anything you do say may be given in evidence.

Action after caution

For persons NOT under arrest and on official premises:

Suspects must be told that they are not under arrest and are not obliged to remain with the officer and that if they choose to stay they may have free legal advice.

For persons NOT under arrest and NOT on official premises:

Suspects must be told that they are not under arrest and are not obliged to remain with the officer. If the suspect then asks about their right to obtain legal advice, they should be told that this right is available.

For persons under arrest:

If caution follows arrest, go straight to the office where the custody officer will deal with initial rights before questioning commences

NOTE: Remember to re-caution prior to questioning commencing or recommencing.

C&E 684   PT(November2001)

The official caution – an aide memoire we kept in our notebooks to make sure we got it right. At 37 words it took some remembering.

Chapter 10

STRIKING GOLD AND GOING SLOW

A s I say, internal concealments were becoming more and more prevalent by the late 1980s. Lots of cannabis resin was being smuggled in this way on flights from Gibraltar and Malaga due to their proximity to Morocco. The usual couriers commonly acquired their gear in Morocco and got the ferry back to Gib or Southern Spain before flying home. As they were generally users themselves a urine test took us no further forward. Therefore if we thought them suspect we nicked them and let nature take its course. Although cannabis didn't have the kudos of a class A drugs seizure, the overtime rate for 'babysitting' a resin swallower was the same, so Malaga and Gibraltar flights were given plenty of attention.

Our best source of internal concealments of class A drugs was the early morning British Airways flight from Lagos in Nigeria and it was on this routing that I got my first stuffer in July 1987. I said earlier that I'd go into more depth about the reasons we stop people; this case was typical of the smugglers we were catching, so offers a good insight.

Most of the couriers we were getting from Lagos fitted a distinct profile. They were generally males travelling on their own between the ages of 20 and 40. They were purportedly here on short business trips to buy goods. They had a smallish amount of British cash and said they had a reservation to stay at a hotel.

A male passenger appeared before me one morning and within a short time my eyes lit up. Peugeot was a very popular make of car in Nigeria at the time and many couriers had said they were coming to the UK to buy spare parts. A lot of our clients also said they would be staying at the Pembury Hotel, which was a bed and breakfast establishment on the Seven Sisters Road.

My opening questions established that he was here for four days to return Peugeot sample parts he'd obtained on his previous visit. He had just £50 in cash and lo and behold he was staying at the Pembury. His passport told me he was just 21 years old but that this was his ninth trip to the UK in the space of 18 months. He was ticking so many boxes that I thought it was too good to be true. I examined his bags and did a search of his person but found nothing. I was still convinced he had to have something so asked if he was prepared to give a urine sample. Although doing this was voluntary, most people agreed to it as they thought to do otherwise would make us think they had something to hide.

His sample was positive for opiates which suggested to us that he had heroin concealed inside him. Heroin was the main type of seizure from Nigeria then although it wasn't long before cocaine supplanted it as the most common class A seizure at Gatwick. With a positive test I arrested him and asked if he had drugs inside him. Sometimes you would find they would crack at this stage and confess. Most times though people continue to deny it in the hope they might still get away with it. My suspect chose this route and so began our war of attrition.

The law at the time only allowed us to detain a suspect without charge for a limited amount of time. We could apply to magistrates to have their time in custody extended if we had sufficient evidence to suspect an offence. It was the following afternoon some 33 hours after his arrest that he cracked while we were waiting to go before the magistrates at Crawley. He had his solicitor with him who had no doubt advised his client that the magistrates weren't about to release him. Rather, they would remand him back to customs until he'd had sufficient bowel movements to prove his innocence. With this information he realised the game was up and decided to come clean. He informed us that he had eleven packages that had been inserted up his rectum with a metal instrument, a pretty painful experience I would've thought.

He said a 'Mr Brown' had done this three hours before his flight at a hotel in Lagos. He was to go to the Pembury Hotel where he would be met and relieved of the contraband. He was told he'd get £500 for his trouble and was only doing it to help his sick father. He was also told the packages contained gold and he stuck to this story when he later pleaded not guilty at court.

The jury obviously didn't think this gold bottomed story was a copper bottomed defence and he was convicted without much deliberation. A not guilty plea by a stuffer or swallower was most unusual. After all, unlike bag jobs, they couldn't really claim that they didn't know it was there. Consequently he got a heftier sentence than he would have got if he had pleaded guilty in the first place. The gold defence was a little ridiculous, and as it was his ninth visit in 18 months I didn't really buy the sick father story either. He'd obviously got away with it a few times already and was getting greedy, the downfall of many shrewder criminals than him.

Although internal concealments were becoming more and more popular there were still many different methods being used. In early 1988 my colleague Sharon Mason found one of the most unusual hiding places I'd see in my career. Giant African land snails were commonly seen in Nigerians' bags. They were considered something of a delicacy in West African communities and lots of them were brought in on the Lagos flight. On this occasion though there was more than snail under the shells of a large consignment that Sharon had found; quite a few had swallower type packages protruding. The smuggler had not accounted for the fact that some of the snails were still alive and as they defrosted from their time in the aircraft hold had started to wriggle. This movement had dislodged the packages from their hiding place and so provided Sharon with a great detection. To be fair our courier could never really have reckoned on a quick getaway.

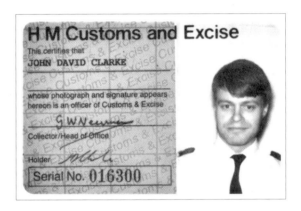

My staff ID card issued soon after my transfer to Gatwick.

Chapter 11

A FABULOUS FORTNIGHT

By 1988 I'd got my feet pretty well under the table at Gatwick. In March that year a second terminal (North) opened and with the expansion in flight movements a whole load of new staff were taken on. Suddenly I was no longer the new boy and with nearly three years at the airport under my belt I felt as though I started to belong. The new influx of staff all had polaroid pictures taken, which were placed on the staff noticeboard with their names and brief pen pictures. The idea was that it would help everyone to get known quicker but all it did was to give people the opportunity to make their own humorous additions. Yours truly was not innocent in this respect and nicknames and other forms of endearment quickly adorned the pictures to ensure the newbies were properly welcomed.

It wasn't only the noticeboard that fell victim to this sort of creativity. A staff address book was kept in the Wendy House, which is what we called our stand-down office adjacent to the green channel. In those days all Sunday shifts were overtime and if somebody couldn't make their rostered shift there was a call out list to make sure that shift didn't go wide. As you can guess, austerity hadn't yet kicked in and there were always plenty of volunteers to work any spare Sundays going. The call out list was managed by a couple of the experienced officers and if you made it to the top of the list you were offered the extra shift. Doctor Sunday was very good at his job though, so it was a rare event to see anyone go sick at a weekend. If people were needed to be called out at short notice it was essential you'd record your name and contact number in the staff address book. However, you don't look a gift horse in the mouth and it was for this reason that it became more commonly known as the staff abuse book. If your name was in there you were there to be shot at and, although some of the additions made weren't necessarily politically correct, they never failed to bring a smile to one's face.

I'd got pretty used to working shifts by then although our roster had some peculiar quirks. To enhance the number of consecutive rest days we had a couple of quick turn rounds. It meant that for a week of nights we worked a day shift on a Friday before we started a run of six nights that same evening. The European working time directive had either not been introduced or had been tacitly ignored. Therefore we worked from 7 until half past 5 before starting back on nights at 11. Unless you lived round the corner there seemed very little point in going home. As a result most teams took the opportunity to indulge in some bonding between shifts which normally took the form of a libation or two in the Foresters in Horley and a Ruby Murray at the Curry Inn.

I started a run of nights on a Friday in late May and on my first morning of the run bagged a swallower from the Lagos flight. Friday nights or Saturday mornings were the opportune time to get one of these into custody as all the babysitting at weekends was on premium rates. What made this even better was that the Monday was the late May Bank Holiday so that was double time too. This event made me very popular with colleagues. As soon as it was known a swallower had been nicked officers on duty formed an orderly queue at the detecting officer's door to offer to babysit. Some liked the extra shifts more than others but it was never too much of a problem to find staff willing to take these shifts off your hands. Consequently the first bit of paperwork completed on arrest was not any legal paraphernalia but the babysitting list. There were a selection of unwritten rules to abide by in the drawing up of this document, though. First of all you looked after yourself and your own team. The remaining gaps would be filled by those you most needed to take care of, in other words officers who were catching swallowers of their own who'd be likely to reciprocate the favour. At the bottom of the list were those that never made any detections of their own, or 'parasites' as they were also known. Although there was a reluctance to dish out any 'gobble' (the term we used for overtime) to these officers there were sometimes so many prisoners in custody that you had no choice.

My chap on that Saturday morning fitted the usual profile at the time. He was here for a week to buy clothing and shoes and was staying at a B & B in Camberwell. The only thing that put me off was that he had over £1,400 in cash which was more than the usual courier would carry. Smugglers tended to be paid cash on delivery so were not normally given too much 'front' money. Nevertheless I decided to give him a spin and within a couple of hours he was perched in our throne room popping out his packages. Double shifts over the ensuing weekend were very handy, as by now I'd bought my first property, a little studio flat just off Sutton High Street. The location was perfect, being close to the station, but more importantly was still only a mile from my mum's washing machine and her Sunday roasts.

By the time this gentleman had produced all his gear and been charged I was pretty exhausted, having filled my boots with overtime. Consequently I wasn't looking too hard when I struck again on the Wednesday morning of the same run of shifts. Again it was a Nigerian chap travelling alone who was here for a week to buy Bedford van spare parts. He only had 400 dollars on him so I felt it would be wrong if I didn't cordially invite him to piss in a pot. A positive result swiftly led to him being asked to extend his stay which he duly did up to and including the following weekend. Terms and conditions were changed within a few years which led to us being paid an annual allowance in return for working antisocial shifts and weekends. Overtime was abolished into the bargain. It's therefore no exaggeration to say that the officers who chased the overtime back in the late 80s and early 90s were earning more than they do today.

As I've alluded to earlier, my adolescence and possibly my obsession with football had not led to much success with the fairer sex. However, this was about to change, and indirectly it came about as a result of my love for the glorious game. England's first game of Euro 88 was against Ireland on the afternoon of Sunday 12th June. The trouble was I was due to be working a late shift and couldn't really afford to turn the double time down. Rescue was at hand when a babysitting shift became available on the Saturday night. I duly got my name down for that and passed up my Sunday late to somebody not so desperate to see the game. Sharon Pears was an assistant officer on a different team and our paths hadn't crossed that often due to the idiosyncrasies of the roster. However, it turned out that she was also working that night to babysit a female swallower we had caught. Sharon came straight in for the shift from a night out and appeared in civvies before getting changed into her uniform. As flattering as the customs uniform was (or more accurately wasn't) I suddenly saw Sharon in a completely different light. We subsequently spent the night together, although it was perfectly innocent sitting in the corridor outside our respective prisoner's cell door. We started to chat and swiftly established a connection that I was keen to explore further. Although strictly speaking it wasn't love at first sight, it was certainly something similar. By the end of the shift I plucked up the courage to ask her out. To my amazement she said yes. It would have capped a perfect fortnight except for the fact that England lost 0-1 that afternoon. Unfortunately there are some things you can rely on.

Chapter 12

JOINING THE BAGGAGE CREWS

England's defeat to Ireland was swiftly followed by two more as they managed to exit Euro 88 in double quick time. My disappointment, though, was assuaged by love as my first date with Sharon was soon followed by several more. I'd already booked a fortnight away with my mates for a lads' holiday in August and Sharon went out to the States to see her dad. It was while I was away that the penny dropped. I was in a club at 6 in the morning allegedly living 'la vida loca' when I thought what the hell am I doing here? I realised that I had a lovely girl waiting for me at home and that perhaps it was time I thought of settling down.

I wasn't sure Sharon would feel the same way so I kept my counsel when I got back home. However, a few weeks later on my way home from my best mate's birthday booze-up I blurted out a marriage proposal. It wasn't a 'down on one knee' moment; I'd have probably struggled to get back up. However, to my delight Sharon said yes although with the caveat that I ask her again when I'd sobered up the next morning. Fortunately she hadn't changed her mind and within three months of going out she was my fiancée.

My life was really on the up. I had my feet on the property ladder, the love of a beautiful woman and a job I loved and was getting increasingly confident at. In November I got another decent drugs job. There were early morning flights from Lagos every day but on Sunday there was also a scheduled teatime arrival. The clientele on this flight seemed slightly different and it was a quite elderly gentleman that I intercepted in the green channel. It turned out he was well in his 60s and very nervous as he immediately asked the way to the toilets when I stopped him. I told him he'd have to wait until I'd looked in his luggage. He had an untagged bag with him which he said was hand luggage, and he stated he hadn't checked any bags in. However, when I told him I wanted to take a look, he said the bag wasn't his. Now I was aware of people using this ruse when it was a checked-in bag, the excuse being that they'd picked up the wrong bag off the carousel. However, as the bag was hand luggage this story was never going to fly. He then pretended not to know the combination to the lock, but it wasn't long before the game was up. Inside were three packages in 'congratulations' wrapping paper and nothing else. It was certainly a nice present for me: 11 kilos of compressed herbal cannabis.

I think this chap was comfortably the eldest courier I ever caught, although I know colleagues who have caught people in their 70s and 80s. Drugs smugglers could come in all shapes and sizes. Certainly, as I said before, a lot would fit a certain profile, but any good organisation would look to recruit couriers that didn't fit the norm. At least the age of this courier meant that if he'd try to do a runner I'd have been reasonably confident of catching him. Contrary to what most people might think it was very rare for anybody to run. I guess it was probably that until the very last moment they'd be hoping that we wouldn't find whatever was being concealed. Running off would have been a sure way to convince us they definitely had something to hide. That's not to say it never happened though. You always needed to remain vigilant and watch people like hawks just in case. After all a cornered animal is the most dangerous.

Like a lot of the couriers I caught I felt quite sorry for this guy especially when I found out how poor and desperate he was.

Whilst he was in prison awaiting his case it was discovered he was suffering with terminal cancer. When it was suggested we drop our case on compassionate grounds I had no hesitation in agreeing. I sincerely hope he got home in time to say farewell to his loved ones.

My next job was back to the usual profile, a Nigerian trader here for a short visit, ostensibly to buy shoes and bags. As she only had £50 on her and her story had more holes than England's defence at that year's Euros, I got her to provide a urine sample. The positive result led to her arrest and, although she held out for 26 hours, nature was the ultimate winner.

Although there were a lot of customs staff at Gatwick spread across Cargo, Tarmac and the baggage hall it was a fairly intimate place in which to work. Most people knew everyone else by virtue of the overlaps on the roster where you were constantly handing over to or relieving different teams. Like most working environments gossip was rife and it was easy to earn yourself a reputation, either good or bad. Fortunately for me I was starting to build quite a good one. Bearing in mind baggage teams had other priorities such as OB, the red channel and more recently the role of custody officer that had been introduced by the Police and Criminal Evidence Act (or PACE as it was better known), the amount of drugs seizures I was making was being noticed. Having said that I was far from the only one. I was still second division compared to some of our staff who seemed to have a sixth sense when it came to finding drugs smugglers. The number of drugs seizures right across the airport was rocketing, and in the spring of 1989 our management decided they would expand the baggage crews to further mine this golden seam. It was suggested to me that I was the type of younger blood they were looking for. Initially I was reluctant to put my name in the frame. I was still a little in awe of some of their number. Quite a few of my peers encouraged me to go for it though, and as

Sharon and I were getting married that September we thought it might provide more opportunities for overtime to help pay for a new house.

My application was accepted and that June I bid a fond farewell to the Green team and joined Ian Colley's fine band of baggage crews. Ian was a lovely guy whose background wasn't particularly drugs based. Although he at times seemed a little overawed by some of the more experienced officers under his command there was no doubt he was held in some affection. He was officially known as Bravo 3 (his radio call sign), but was more commonly known as Shep or the Blackpool Bootboy, having let us in on his love for his boyhood football team. There were three teams of baggage crews each of which had been expanded to eight staff comprised of four pairs of officers. A few of us new boys started at the same time so we were each paired with one of the experienced hands. Keith Tatler was to be my partner and to say he was a character would be an understatement. I was to go on to have much success and fun with him. Simon Hart was a similar age to me when he joined and he was paired with Geoff Williams who was a Gatwick legend and who remains a good friend to this day. Although we worked as pairs the four of us quickly built a good rapport, and if your partner wasn't in you tagged along with the other pair. The great thing about the baggage crews was that drugs were your only priority. Furthermore you were pretty much given autonomy to work how and where you liked. Of course there was more pressure on you to find drugs but it was to be a pressure on which I thrived.

Chapter 13

HITTING THE GROUND RUNNING

Within the first month of working together, my partner Keith Tatler got two swallowers. I'd like to say it was my youthful enthusiasm rubbing off on him but Tatty was a very able and experienced officer who probably thought he'd show the new boy he still had it. As his partner I was one of the first invitees to the overtime party so it was all good. Tatty's success was making me more eager, though, to get something of my own to prove I was worthy of my place on the baggage crews. Fortunately I didn't have to wait too long, as a couple of weeks later I got a swallower of my own on a Saturday morning Lagos flight.

I'd taken up position waiting behind the immigration desks when a very smiley gentleman hove into view with a British Airways ID around his neck. He explained that he worked for the airline as a ticketing officer in Nigeria but was here privately to collect Peugeot spare parts. The spare parts profile had come up numerous times and he had no need to have his British Airways ID on show. I thought he was probably wearing it as a distraction and to enhance his credibility as a bona fide visitor. His happy demeanour also seemed a little too much and was, I thought, more a nervous reaction than genuine.

My instinct was to prove right and a few hours later after a positive urine test he started to produce packages. He was typical of most people we caught in the sense that once they'd been arrested they were extremely compliant and model detainees.

Perhaps it was because we treated them with respect and courtesy, something they weren't necessarily used to in their previous dealings with the law. It did turn out to be true that he worked for British Airways and during his stay with us he asked if it would be alright for his wife to visit him. He said she could get a cheap staff ticket over from Nigeria. Although it was highly unusual to allow visits, we got authority from our management that a supervised visit would be permitted. At that time courts weren't sitting at weekends so if a swallower hadn't gone clear by a Friday afternoon we couldn't put them into the system for remand to prison until a Monday morning.

I think the thought of a visit from his wife led to a very sedate delivery of his packages. We were hardly complaining as every day he spent in our company meant more overtime. His wife got booked on the next Saturday morning flight, fully seven days after her husband's arrival. Packages were being passed in a trickle rather than the usual flood and it was only after court had closed on Friday that the first clear bowel movement was produced. It meant he would have to stay the weekend which was a win-win situation. Double time for us and a visit from his wife for him. As we knew he was now clear of packages, and possibly as a reward for his model behaviour, his visit from his wife was perhaps not as strictly supervised as it could have been. After all it was going to be a few years before he'd see her again.

Within a week I had another job as a result of a colleague's detection. Brian Gamble was part of the other half of Ian Colley's team and he'd picked out a Nigerian in transit to Dallas who'd confessed after giving a positive urine sample. We were having a lot of success with couriers transiting to the USA at the time, many of whom claimed to be working as cab drivers there. One of Tatty's swallowers from the previous month had been travelling as part of a pair so I had a hunch that Brian's chap might not be on his own. I quickly shot round to the British Airways desk to find out if any other passengers were transiting from Lagos to Dallas, and to my satisfaction I was given the name of another traveller. Not only that but there was a chap waiting furtively near the counter who turned out to be that very man. Bingo, I thought, and a short while later he was reunited with his pal at the custody suite and an extended spell at Her Majesty's pleasure thereafter.

In the August I got my hat trick with yet another swallower off the Lagos. Three jobs in three months had justified my decision to join the baggage crews and with my wedding a month away the overtime was coming in very handy. Having made so many friends at the airport I'd decided I needed to have a separate stag do for them in addition to the one for my mates in Sutton. There was going to be a lot of ale to pay for which indirectly was being funded by the proceeds of drug trafficking.

On 16th September 1989, with many of our colleagues in attendance, Sharon and I tied the knot. It was a perfect sunny day and I felt blessed to have married such a lovely woman. I knew my luck was in that day; even Fulham won.

Chapter 14

SETTLING DOWN

After a dream wedding and a fabulous honeymoon in Acapulco we returned to complete our purchase of a maisonette in Sutton, our first home together. Having missed a few of our rostered weekends while we were away we were both grateful that so many swallowers were being caught at Gatwick. It meant that on our return to work there was plenty of overtime to be had. Sharon was more in demand than me in that respect. Woman couriers were just as prevalent but there were far more male customs officers than females. Male officers could help babysit female prisoners but were obviously not allowed to be present when they passed packages. Consequently if we had women prisoners our female staff were in constant demand to babysit.

As the baggage crews were getting most of the drugs jobs, I was getting offered plenty of overtime on the basis I was now one of their own, and Sharon was being equally well looked after by proxy. In actual fact we started to turn down a lot of the shifts we were offered so that we could get some quality time off. There was so much overtime on offer that it was easy to get greedy. A couple of officers were notorious for grabbing every shift going to the extent that they eventually got exhausted and very ill. This was one of the reasons why ultimately the overtime system was abolished and babysitting was done by those on duty instead. It also meant that the department saved a lot of money, which was probably a bigger factor in the decision.

I was soon having success of my own again. A nice little herbal cannabis job from Jamaica in November was followed by three in a week in December. The first of these I was particularly chuffed with, as on first glance the man I'd stopped was extremely plausible. He stated he was here from Nigeria to buy pharmaceuticals and the paperwork he was carrying looked genuine enough. What's more he had £6,000 in cash with him, far more than we'd expect any courier to be carrying. However, the stamps in his passport showed this was his 11th trip here in two years and he did say he was staying at the Pembury, a venue we associated with many of our seizures. I thought that, even if his business was genuine, he might be supplementing it with a less wholesome activity. Forty-three swallowed packages of heroin proved me right. To add insult to injury the judge later rejected his claim that the six grand was legitimate business money and confiscated it as the proceeds of drug trafficking.

Two days later I got a Ghanaian woman from Accra whose story was so poor that immigration weren't prepared to stamp her in. I'd been listening behind the desk and said I'd be happy to take her off their hands for a search. Her bags were clean, so I asked Sharon (who happened to be on duty) if she would search her and get a urine sample. I heard a kerfuffle from outside the search room and Sharon emerged to say that in giving the sample the woman had decided to pee all over the floor. Proof if any were needed that the job wasn't all glamour and that she most definitely had something to hide. Sharon had been quick enough to retrieve enough urine to do a test, which to no great surprise was positive. The woman went on to pass 43 packages; it was my lucky number that week

The hat trick seizure arrived from New York at the end of the week in the form of a gentleman carrying a steel double drum. It made sweet music for me as, when we took it apart, we found it was stuffed with packages of herbal cannabis. It was the weight that gave it away. The drum weighed almost four kilos and nearly 3 kilos of that was the drugs. It would've been a very good concealment but greed had given it away; this was often the case. Very slick and professional concealments were let down by the fact that too much product was inside.

Up to now all the drugs seizures I'd made had been as the result of 'cold pulls'. This was the term we used for interceptions made without any prior information. In fact early in my career this was pretty much all we did, as intelligence gathering and prior information was in its infancy. We did have an investigation unit on station and often if they were available we'd run a job live. By this I mean that we would not inform the passenger we'd found drugs but allow them to proceed. We would have held them up long enough to have our plain clothes investigators on hand who would follow them out on to the concourse and arrest any meeters or greeters as well. They too would then be interviewed to see if they could be implicated in the offence.

Further afield we had the Investigation Division which was where I'd started my career. They had specialist drugs teams who weren't so interested in the small fry that we were catching at the airport. Their targets were the organisers who were much higher up the chain and who were the criminals making serious money from drug trafficking, unlike the couriers who got a comparative pittance. It was thanks to the I D that I had my next job handed to me on a plate. They were investigating a gang bringing in cocaine from Jamaica and had the name of a courier they expected to bring in the next consignment. They even knew the expected method of concealment – in the soles of shoes. My job was simply to intercept the guy and get him to confirm ownership of his bags and their contents and then let him go. The bloke's look of relief was in stark contrast to how he looked a short while later when our investigators brought him back in along with the guy who'd met him. I then got to examine his bags properly and sure enough in two pairs of shoes I found packages of coke. Any protestations of innocence were rather spoiled by the fact there was coke in the shoes he had on as well.

The investigators thanked me for my help and then took the chap off my hands. I can only assume they busted this courier as they were very close to taking out the principals of this organisation. However, this information was understandably on a 'need to know' basis and wasn't going to be shared with a humble bag opener like me.

A leather bound voluminous anti-smuggling guide issued to all Gatwick staff. Think this was pre-austerity days…

Chapter 15

GETTING LUCKY

I said earlier that finding drugs was a lot down to just being in the right place at the right time. The way I worked never changed that much in the sense that I hit the flights that were proving most fruitful on a regular basis. That's not to say we weren't looking at lower risk flights. If you didn't, there was no way you would identify new trends. Good couriers would look for circuitous routes into the UK to increase their chances. Therefore we often looked at flights from European hubs to see if we could find people connecting from drugs source countries. Our bread and butter though came from the highest risk origins, and so you would concentrate your efforts there. Even so, if your luck was out, you could go months without making a seizure. For some reason my success came in spates and it was important to ride the wave while your luck was in.

After the three in a week before Christmas I managed to get two seizures in successive days in February. My information-based job had been in shoes and at this time it was proving the most popular method of concealment. We were working in a very competitive environment so officers were keen to take the first chance of making a detection. Once, I enquired about the shoes a chap was wearing as soon as he'd passed the immigration control, only for him to tell me two people in the same uniform as me had already searched his shoes as he got off the plane.

I was lucky enough to get a chap from Guyana one morning who hadn't already been accosted by a colleague. He said he was here for two months to see the sights although he couldn't name any of the attractions he wanted to see. I thought the story was cobblers which was apt, as the shoes he had on had a package of coke in each heel. A second London bus arrived in quick succession a day later with an identical concealment on a gent arriving from Jamaica. Jobs like this on the person were straightforward to knock off, as invariably the punter would confess. If it was on the body, particularly where the gear was strapped round them or if it was secreted in underwear, then it was pretty implausible to say you didn't know it was there. Drugs concealed in baggage could be a different kettle of fish though. Even if they'd admitted they'd packed the bag when stopped in the green channel, they could wriggle when interviewed. They would often say somebody else must've got to the bag and put the stuff in there. Notwithstanding this, a denial on the day didn't always equate to a not guilty plea in court. When people realised how unlikely their stories sounded in the cold light of day, they tended to put their hands up, especially as a guilty plea meant a lesser sentence.

I caught another Nigerian swallower in April which didn't owe too much to chance, but the next seizure I got had jam written all over it. As I wrote earlier, Euro 88 had been a disaster for England. Bobby Robson had been considered fortunate by some to keep his job. He had redeemed himself by getting us through the World Cup qualifiers, though, and hope was springing eternal as we flew off to Italia 90. We drew our first two group games so were left with a winner-takes-all match with Egypt. The bad news was I was on shift that day. The good news was that our rest room had a TV, and the room was spookily well populated when the game began. As a conscientious soul I thought I'd better do some work when the first half ended. My old mate Geoff Williams came with me and as we wandered into the baggage hall we saw a bag with a rush tag next to the carousel for a flight from Amsterdam. Rush tags are put on bags that have missed a connection that the passenger made and put on the next available flight to that destination.

From the tag we could see the bag had originally come from Pakistan. As a source country for heroin we thought we ought to take a closer look, especially as it was a Samsonite hardsider we'd been finding false bottoms in. We took the case to our x-ray machine in the green channel but the image was inconclusive. I therefore stuck my knife in and withdrew it to find brown powder on the blade. Geoff tested it and lo and behold we had a heroin seizure. We went to the baggage enquiries desk and from the tag number they were able to tell us the name and address of the person who'd reported the bag missing. The passenger had even completed a customs form for the bag in which they stated they had nothing to declare. In fairness they were hardly likely to write on the form that they had five kilos of heroin.

We alerted our investigation unit to the find and the following day they made a controlled delivery of the bag which resulted in a number of arrests and the breaking up of a major organisation. As for me and Geoff, we made it back to the rest room for the end of the second half where we got luckier still; England actually won.

Chapter 16

FAMILY MAN

My hot streak had to dry up some time, and after Geoff and I had stumbled over that bag of heroin I hit a really lean spell, as did a lot of my colleagues. We'd had such success on the Lagos flight that we pretty much killed the goose that laid the golden egg. Drug smugglers aren't stupid; they were obviously having too much of their product taken out at Gatwick so must have started to look for other routings. However, as jobs from Nigeria started to dry up we were starting to find more and more gear coming in from the Caribbean. Yardie gang culture was getting big in the UK and they were heavily into the drug trade. Originally we were mainly getting herbal cannabis jobs but as the 90s progressed we were finding more and more cocaine on these flights. The various islands were being used as staging posts for coke which was predominantly being produced by the cartels in Colombia. It was a while before I had any decent detections on these routings, although it wasn't for the want of trying.

It turned out that success for me was lying in a different area. I'd settled happily into married life with Sharon and as 1990 closed we were heading off to a new year's eve party at my best mate's house. Before we went I asked Sharon if she was going to make a new year's resolution. She said her wish for 1991 was to have a baby. We'd already agreed that we wanted children so I was only too happy to go along with the idea. We had a short break in Madrid that spring and when I got home from work the day after we got back Sharon said I'd better sit down as she had some news for me. I have to say she had me a little worried until she produced the test kit from Boots that confirmed she was pregnant. I couldn't quite believe it had happened so quickly. If only Fulham could hit the target so easily, my trips to Craven Cottage would be a lot happier.

The upstairs maisonette we were in wasn't really ideal for bringing up children, so we started house hunting immediately. Prices were soaring so getting anything close to the airport was going to be a struggle. Ultimately we found a new-build three bedroom house near Littlehampton on the south coast. Sharon's mum was in Worthing so it was nice for them to be close and prices were much cheaper than the equivalent near Gatwick.

In June I finally broke my famine with a job on my tried and trusted flight from Lagos. Although it wasn't producing as much there was still the odd bit of success to be had, so I'd taken up position in the immigration hall to listen to the stories from the latest arrivals. One chap wasn't able to satisfy the immigration officer, so I said I'd take him off their hands to turn his bags out. The passenger said he didn't have any checked-in luggage so I took him directly to the customs hall to examine his bags. In his briefcase was a plastic wallet containing what looked like four brand new suitcase keys which he said were for his case at home. He was adamant that he had no checked-in bags. This story didn't take long to unravel when I found baggage tag receipts for two pieces of luggage. Closer examination of his ticket also showed that he had checked in two pieces weighing 40 kilos.

I took him to the reclaim belt and sure enough there was one hardsided suitcase left on the carousel with a tag number which matched one of the receipts in his possession. I took him back to the green channel with the case where I played Prince Charming to his Cinderella. I didn't have a glass slipper but I did have a key that fitted his suitcase perfectly. Once opened it proved to be full of herbal cannabis. The mystery of the other bag he'd checked in was soon cleared up as well, as my old mate Sleasy Parisi had stopped a woman on the same flight with an identical brand of suitcase. This bore the bag tag number for the other receipt he had and as you can no doubt guess was opened by one of the four keys he was carrying and was also full of wacky baccy. Our two guests were jointly charged later that day with conspiring to import cannabis which was a satisfactory way to end my drought. It also underlined the importance of having a suspicious mind and of thoroughly examining paperwork. Like a lot of the revenue seizures I'd made, they were often given away by the fact that the passenger hadn't thrown the receipt for the goods away. This chap had tried to pretend he had no checked-in bags but had made the mistake of not throwing the bag tag receipts away. What's more my suspicious or perhaps cynical nature didn't believe his claim about the suitcase keys being for a case he'd left at home. In my experience I'd often have people with cases they'd claimed to have mislaid the key for; it was never likely to happen the other way round.

Back at home we'd found out that our baby was due in November but it was really going to be cutting it fine to be in our new house in time. As it turned out we made it with nine days to spare and on 17th November 1991 our son Daniel made his entrance into the world. Sharon started labour on the Saturday morning but Daniel played very hard to get, and it was just after 10am the next morning before he finally made his appearance. It was perfect timing really as it was my rostered Sunday off, so I didn't even lose any double time. In fairness though, like all kids he's cost me a few quid since.

Chapter 17

THE TALKING MATTRESS

If there was one thing you could be sure of in my job it was that no change was no option. I've gone from HM Customs and Excise to HM Revenue and Customs to the UK Border Agency to the UK Border Force over my career whilst ostensibly doing exactly the same job. I'm sure it's no different in the private sector and I appreciate that, as times change, it's wise to review how you operate. However, I've always been an advocate of the maxim 'If it's not broken don't fix it.'

In 1991 there was a fundamental review of how we should be organised. When I started at the airport a lot of terminology still referred to us as preventive officers. Our presence was as important to deter and prevent smuggling as it was to seize contraband. A lot of would-be smugglers are put off by the threat of being caught, in the same way that speeding motorists slow down in the presence of a speed camera. The preventive effect could not be scientifically measured though, and so as times changed a target culture developed. Schools and hospitals have gone that way too and are now put into nice neat league tables each year. Greater minds than mine could more readily debate whether this has occasioned any actual improvement in performance, but it's a cultural shift that we've all had to get used to.

The review into our job took place and it was decided that the baggage crews were to be done away with. I thought that we were being very successful and I'm not certain too many of the grass roots were consulted in the process. Perhaps they thought our methods were a little archaic and didn't fit in with the more modern 'intelligence led' culture. I'd argue that a lot of the intelligence was acquired from good 'cold pull' interceptions in the first place, but then that's only my opinion.

Some of the crews moved into intelligence and profiling but for me it was back to the future as the remainder of us were absorbed back into baggage teams. Although Keith Tatler had been my original partner on the crews, circumstances ended up with me being paired with Geoff Williams most of the time. Although Geoff was about 15 years my senior we clicked immediately and built a great rapport over the years. Happily when I went back on a team, Geoff got on the same one and our relationship continued.

Geoff had a multitude of stories from his earlier days and laughter was never far away when we worked together. He told me that on one occasion he'd stopped a 'captain of industry' who thought it was beneath him to be stopped by Customs. His superior 'I pay your wages' attitude was not going down well with Geoff who finished the encounter by telling the chap to go forth and multiply. This unsurprisingly went down like a lead balloon and he demanded to speak to the senior officer on duty. This happened to be the imposing figure of Johnny Johnson, who was an ex-military policeman. 'What appears to be the problem, Sir?' he politely enquired. 'Your officer has just told me to fuck off!' Johnny considered the position carefully before replying, 'Then with all due respect, sir, why don't you?' The gentleman quickly assessed that Johnny was not the sort of guy you should argue with and departed the scene without further ado.

I was well aware that in those days stories like this weren't that unusual. Geoff told me of a colleague who'd come back from a very hospitable meal break to work in the red channel. He'd started looking in a passenger's case at the top of which was a very comfortable looking bath towel. He obviously decided to inspect this item very closely as a moment later the passenger said to Geoff, 'Your colleague appears to be asleep in my suitcase, sir.' Perhaps this officer introduced what we know today as the power nap...

Geoff had me in stitches many times. Once I went in as a witness on a search of a suspect coming in from Amsterdam. Each search room could double as a cell so there was a mattress on the bench. Some of the lining had split on this particular mattress which left a small air pocket which when the chap sat down on it made a large noise not dissimilar to that of a fart. 'Been eating beans have we, sir?' said Geoff in a deadpan manner. It took all of my professionalism not to dissolve into laughter. This search room was forever after known as the one with the 'talking mattress'. I was certainly reluctant to do any more searches with Geoff in that room.

On another occasion he'd caught a Nigerian woman on crutches who turned out to have cannabis in her luggage. In the interview she confessed and said that her injury had forced her out of work and so she had been forced to smuggle for the money. Geoff responded in blissful ignorance, 'So you're saying you've done it to stand on your own two feet.' This time my professionalism started to crack and I quickly stopped the tape and got Geoff to step out of the interview room. Geoff was nonplussed until I pointed out the unintended irony of his comment. It was a few minutes before we were composed enough to return.

Geoff and I both had a good general knowledge and in our breaks we would supplement our income playing the trivia machines dotted around the airport. We did very nicely and on occasions attracted a few colleagues along. On one occasion Keith Tatler was with us and put his radio in the winnings tray of the machine. We obviously were out of luck that time as we were on the transit back to the other terminal before Tatty realised he'd left his radio behind. He probably never moved as fast in his career as he made the return trip in double quick time. Fortunately for him his radio was where he'd left it. The loss of such an expensive piece of kit in those circumstances would have taken some explaining.

A few years later Sharon saw an advert in the paper for auditions for a new BBC quiz show, and suggested that Geoff and I should go for it. We duly did so and ended up on Martyn Lewis's 'Today's the Day' which was filmed in Manchester. We travelled up the day before and had a good night out the evening before filming. The make-up ladies certainly earned their money that morning. It was a really good experience and we did manage to beat the reigning winners who ultimately came back to win the overall series prize. It was probably a blessing that we were beaten by the next pair. If we'd won, we'd have had to stay another night up there. Good news for Manchester's hostelries maybe, but not for our health.

One of the biggest let-downs of my career. I'd been required to give evidence in New York for a transit job we'd let run from Lagos to JFK. This is my embassy ID pass from when I went to get an advance for expenses...then two days before the trip the bastard changed his plea to guilty! Furthest trip I ever got in the job was searching a shipping container in Cleethorpes – not quite the same.

Chapter 18

TRENDY SHOES AND UNDIES

As seizures from West Africa started to dry up, finds on flights from the Caribbean rocketed. Although internal concealments had become the most common modus operandi from Nigeria and Ghana they were less common at that time from the Caribbean. They were still using traditional but at times ingenious methods of concealment. Anne Paterson, a colleague on my new team, had a particularly brilliant detection on a woman coming back from Kingston. Although she said she was unemployed it was her second trip to Jamaica in a matter of months, so Anne took a close interest in her luggage. Amongst a myriad of foodstuff was a large bag of what the lady claimed were nutmegs. Anne took a closer look and thought she could see dried glue on some of the husks. We chiselled our way through the shells and lo and behold inside was white powder which reacted positively for cocaine. This was a great job as they hadn't tried to be greedy. Forty-eight nutmegs produced just over 130 grams of coke, enough to make the run worthwhile but not so much to make it obvious.

Anne's find was top-notch and was relayed to our staff in case it was the start of a new trend. Every bag of nutmegs or the like was taken apart for months afterwards, but I think Anne's find was a one-off. We were getting lots of cocaine in solution jobs, though. The coke would be dissolved in bottles of liquid, commonly labelled as ginger wine or dark rum. If the courier got through, the gear could be retrieved by means of the evaporation process. The most common method used in this period was still on the body, though, normally in the shoes being worn but often too in packages concealed in underwear.

This method was responsible for my next hat trick of seizures although each courier gave a different reason for their trip. The first was on a man from Guyana who said he was a professional boxer. He was supposedly here for a week to buy clothing and shoes, but also had a ticket for a flight to Geneva where he said he was meeting a boxing promoter to arrange a bout. As he was pretty vague about his arrangements I decided he warranted a search. The shoes he was wearing contained cocaine and aptly for a boxer he had another package in (you've guessed it) his boxers. Another sportsman provided my next job. A young Londoner had been to Jamaica for three weeks to see family and he claimed he was a semi pro footballer with a well known non-league club in south London. The trouble for him was that I was quite familiar with the team he was talking about and I told him I'd never heard of him. Let him down gently, I thought. He then said he was in the reserve team and earned £10 a game but was otherwise unemployed. Alarm bells rang for two reasons. Based on his income it was highly unlikely he'd funded his own trip, and secondly, if he was serious about making strides as a footballer, he wouldn't have taken a three-week holiday in the middle of the season. Another trip to the search room beckoned and sure enough a short while later I had another coke concealment in shoes. The poor chap's breakthrough to the first team would have to wait, although he'd probably have been a shoe-in for the prison football team.

My next job was thanks to an ex-baggage crew colleague, Brian Gamble, who had moved on to a profiling team. They would work in plain clothes, typically at the gates on departing flights to high risk areas such as the Caribbean. There they would casually chat to passengers about the trips they were going on to see who might be worthy of a tug on the way back. They wouldn't disclose who they worked for, so as not to spook any would-be courier; if ever asked they'd generally answer that they were carrying out surveys for the airport or airlines. Brian had been a very successful detection officer so knew exactly who to be looking out for. He told me he had spoken to a Glaswegian on an outbound flight to St Lucia who said he was only going for a week for a music festival. The profilers were very adept at remembering names and dates of birth from just a quick look at someone's passport. This enabled them to do more extensive checks back at the office. Brian was therefore able to tell me that this was the man's second trip to the Caribbean in three weeks. Brian didn't think he seemed to be the sort to afford such extravagance so he was definitely worthy of close attention on his return.

On interception the chap duplicated the story he'd told Brian but had no credible explanation for the earlier trip. When I said I wanted to search him he exercised his rights of appeal and said he wanted to be heard by the magistrates. Although it was his right I felt it was more because he had something to hide than any burning sense of injustice at his treatment. A hearing took a little while to arrange and included calling out the duty solicitor on his behalf who said he would meet us at court. Once he'd spoken to his brief he called us over and confessed he had a kilo of coke on him, in the form of four packages in his underwear and a concealment in his shoes. The solicitor had obviously told him there was no chance the magistrates would uphold his objection to the search so he decided to stop delaying the inevitable. Brian's instincts had proved correct, as did many of my colleagues who'd moved across to profiling and who for many years would provide the leads to lots of the drug seizures at the airport.

Chapter 19

WHAT A TANGLED WEB IS WEAVED

Sharon and I had settled into our new house nicely and were enjoying the responsibility of being parents. She had taken a career break from work to look after Daniel and it wasn't long before she fell pregnant again. Bethany was born in June 1993 and again, fortunately for the Clarke finances, she arrived on my rostered Sunday off. This was particularly handy as by now we were being switched to an annualised hours contract that proved the death knell for any extra overtime. With two little mouths to feed and Sharon at home I was eager to earn as much as possible but having moved off the baggage crews there wasn't as much potential to make seizures as before.

When overtime was abolished and babysitting of prisoners was done within shift, this also seemed to have a negative effect on the amount of seizures being made. It may have been a coincidence but Margaret Thatcher's earlier abolition of seizure rewards had achieved the same effect. Money was far from our only motivation. In those days drugs were still very high in the public's consciousness and we felt that what we were doing in customs work was very important and was valued by the government and broader society. However, it's human nature to be motivated by incentives and as pay went down it was not altogether surprising that the amount of seizures seemed to head the same way.

Having said that there were still plenty of jobs to be had and in September I picked up a swallower from Nigeria who had proffered a story that fitted the time honoured profile. Where he differed was that once he'd provided a positive urine sample, he coughed and admitted he had swallowed straight away. He was probably feeling the pressure as over the next couple of days he passed a total of exactly 100 packages. This was at the higher end of the tariff. Obviously a courier's capacity was determined to some extent by their physique but a three figure score was pretty unusual.

The following month produced a nice double-hander from Jamaica when a colleague and I took a shine to two ladies who came through the immigration controls separately and who both said they were travelling alone. They both gave similar stories about being here to buy clothing and both had similar amounts of money. Immigration weren't satisfied, so my mate and I took them off their hands to do a search. Once we dug a little deeper our interest was piqued still further. Both of their airline tickets had been bought at the same travel agent, their departure tax receipts in Kingston were just three numbers apart and lo and behold they had sat next to each other on the plane. They still continued to deny knowledge of each other, though, which only made us more suspicious. Nothing was found in their bags or on their person but a positive urine test and then x-ray revealed they both had packages stuffed in their vaginas.

The packages were identically shaped and wrapped, and when the drugs were analysed by the government chemist the cocaine was found to be of identical purity. They were therefore jointly charged and subsequently convicted. Had they admitted from the start that they were together they might have had a better chance of getting through, but once they were caught in a lie I guess they thought they had to see it through.

Lying is inherently more difficult than telling the truth and often makes the hole you're in even deeper. This was true of the next seizure I made, although to be fair this woman was far more plausible. She was a young English woman who had returned from Jamaica via Miami with about 400 grams of cocaine in the trainers she was wearing. On the day, she completely denied knowledge of the drugs and said someone must have tampered with her shoes when she'd left them in the place she was staying. She couldn't offer a credible explanation about how she didn't realise the difference in weight when she put them on for the trip home, nor what she would have done if she had discovered the drugs in them. Therefore when she got to court for her trial she came up with a better story and offered a defence of duress. She said an ex-boyfriend of hers had threatened her and her family, unless she agreed to smuggle drugs for him. She said that when she had been going out with him she had no idea he was a violent criminal, but said by the time he got her to do the drugs run she was terrified of him. The jury couldn't decide either way whether she was being truthful and were unable to reach a verdict. For the only time in my career I had a case going to re-trial.

Fortunately this gave us the opportunity to look into the boyfriend and with the police's assistance we were able to discredit our girl's story. There was no doubt the man was a violent criminal and had just been convicted for the attempted murder of two policemen he'd shot in London, for which he'd been sentenced to 25 years in prison. Indeed he'd also been arrested in the USA for attempted murder and he'd been deported from there to stand trial.

The key thing the police told us was that our girl had given alibi evidence on his behalf when he'd been accused of armed robbery some two years before when she'd supposedly been going out with him. It put a big hole in her contention that she had no idea of his violent nature. The police also confirmed to me that a photo she had in her handbag was a picture of him which didn't ring true if she was in genuine fear of him. We also got the film from her camera developed which seemed to show a girl having the time of her life on holiday in Jamaica rather than someone living in terror.

We were able to put all this evidence forward at the re-trial and this time the jury took just over an hour to record a unanimous guilty verdict. I took no great pleasure in seeing a young woman incarcerated but to me it was satisfying that the work we'd done in proving our case had paid off. Rightly or wrongly I felt that when giving evidence I was being judged as well. In that sense I was always happy when the verdict went in our favour.

Over my career far more people I caught pleaded guilty than went to trial. No doubt they were advised that they'd receive a shorter sentence by not taking up court time, but mainly in the cold light of day most people take responsibility for their actions. I've often read media stories about young Brits abroad being 'duped' into carrying drugs and ending up unjustly in foreign jails. I may be cynical but I never believe much in their innocence. All the smugglers I caught that went to trial were found guilty. I'm not saying that just to blow my own trumpet. It's just that most people struggle to believe in the concept that truly innocent people have somehow been hoodwinked into carrying something they know nothing about.

Chapter 20

PERSONAL TRAGEDY

With quite a few years experience under my belt I was now being given the opportunity to act as team leader when the permanent boss was away or on leave. In those days the team senior officer wore civilian dress to differentiate themselves and possibly look more neutral when they were called upon to authorise searches of person or adjudicate on offences. Therefore the old wedding suit got dusted off and was aired on quite a few occasions. Although I quite enjoyed the responsibility I missed the cut and thrust of doing regular interceptions myself.

I did apply for permanent promotion and got as far as an interview board before being rejected. I wasn't that heartbroken. At that time if you made Higher Executive Officer grade it was almost certain it would be in a non shift post away from the airport, which would have occasioned a substantial drop in pay. With a young family to support I was glad it wasn't a decision I had to make.

Back on the shop floor I got another spate of seizures on what was by now our most fertile source, the Caribbean. A Brit coming back from Grenada, with his wife and child as cover, turned out to have a kilo of coke in his underpants. Then a 20-year-old Londoner came back from Jamaica with half a kilo in her bra and pants. She made a full and frank confession and her age meant she served her sentence at a young offenders institute rather than prison.

Jamaica was also the source of about 400 grams of herbal cannabis wrapped in a pair of jeans in a man's suitcase. He had been presented to me by immigration who were concerned that he was travelling on a doctored British passport. The bloke was doubly unlucky as not only was he caught with the drugs but immigration discovered he was a Jamaican national who was subject to deportation. He had substituted his photograph into a genuine British passport that he'd fraudulently acquired.

I then picked up another two kilos of cannabis in the false bottom of a holdall that a young British guy was carrying back from Jamaica. As the nineties progressed more and more of our drug seizures came from the Caribbean, particularly Jamaica. As we entered the new millennium we were at times inundated with drug couriers and particularly swallowers from there, which was proving an untenable demand on our resources. It led indirectly to the requirement that Jamaican nationals would have to get pre-entry visas to come to the UK. This legislation was introduced in 2003 and made a significant difference, as it made it less simple to recruit couriers. We also cut off a lot of the problem at source by sending teams of officers to the Caribbean to assist local authorities to identify smugglers and take the drugs out at that end. These operations have enjoyed much success over the years.

By now my wife Sharon had come back to work part-time, as our sister-in-law was a childminder and was able to take care of the kids. Life was going well and we were looking to move to a new house when tragedy struck. We had been due to visit friends on a Saturday at the end of September 1996 but Sharon felt too unwell to travel. When she was no better by the Monday I took her to the doctor who diagnosed an inner ear infection. By the Wednesday she was in such pain that our doctor got her admitted to hospital. On the Thursday she was given a CT scan which I'd assumed was purely routine. However, when that evening a doctor approached her bed and said he'd like to take us to a private room for a chat, my heart started to fill with dread. He showed us the image from the scan which indicated that Sharon had a large tumour in her brain. Until then I'd had no idea what the symptoms of shock were but it was no exaggeration to say that I felt like my very insides had been sucked away.

Sharon was transferred to a specialist neurological unit the next day where a biopsy proved the tumour was malignant. Sharon underwent radiotherapy which did buy some time. It was after one session of treatment that we found out that her tumour was of the most aggressive strain with the worst sort of prognosis. We shed bucket loads of tears that day but my darling wife was so strong mentally. She had an inner faith and refused to feel sorry for herself and so we just concentrated on living. The treatment bought precious time and we managed to take the kids to Euro Disney in the spring of 1997. By the end of summer, though, she was going downhill fast. She then came under the care of St Barnabas Hospice in Worthing, which provided the most special and caring environment. She succumbed to the illness on 5th November 1997; Bethany had been four that June and Daniel was just short of his sixth birthday.

As awful as that time was, I only have praise for the way I was treated at work. Everybody knew what we were going through and I was given as much time off as I needed to help care for Sharon and the children. They knew we were both conscientious workers. Sharon even attended court to give evidence on a drugs seizure she had made shortly after her first course of treatment. The defence solicitors had been made aware of her condition but refused to allow Sharon's evidence to be read in her absence. I hope the person who made that call can live with themself.

Huge numbers of colleagues came to Sharon's funeral, and my own boss told me I was only to come back to work when I was ready. The fact was that staying at home was not going to make the grief any less, so a couple of weeks later I returned on a part-time basis when my sister-in-law could have the kids. It was difficult at first as people didn't know what to do or say around me. I told my boss to put the word out that they should stop walking on eggshells around me. If I needed a cry I told them I would head somewhere quiet, but otherwise I wanted a little bit of normality back in my life. I wouldn't say it was back to the usual banter straight away but being at work with good friends was a source of great comfort to me.

Over the years I've become known for my sense of humour at Gatwick. Colleagues would no doubt attest to hearing my repertoire at least half a dozen times. Every workplace can feel special if the atmosphere is right but I can truly say I've felt privileged to have spent nearly all my working life in Gatwick Customs. When I was at my lowest ebb, people were there for me, and the camaraderie and fun I've enjoyed over such a long period make me feel truly blessed.

Chapter 21

BACK TO WORK

Within a couple of weeks of returning to work I got a really nice seizure of cocaine off the British Airways flight from Caracas in Venezuela. South America was the source of most of the cocaine coming to this country. Pablo Escobar and the Medellin cartel in Colombia were infamous as being central to the narcotics trade. Most of their drugs were routed through staging posts, hence we were getting so much success on flights from the different Caribbean islands. However, we were obviously interested in any direct flights as well. For a spell we had an Avianca flight from Bogota to Gatwick. So much trade was expected from that flight that we were given basic Spanish lessons to help us with our questioning. This flight was short-lived, though, as was the BA flight direct from Caracas. As so often with seizures, I just happened to be in the right place at the right time to deal with a chap on a Venezuelan passport claiming to be in transit to Sweden for a Christmas holiday.

Fortunately for me his English was very good so I didn't have to employ my pidgin Spanish when I intercepted him. His command of the language and general demeanour meant I was reasonably convinced of his credibility. However, he only had one small hard-sided case with him, of a type commonly used to conceal drugs. My interest grew further once I'd removed the contents as it still seemed heavier than you'd expect an empty case to be. The next step was to spike the bottom which when I removed it had telltale white powder on the end. A quick drugs field test unsurprisingly proved positive for coke and hey presto a nice result was achieved.

There were over two kilos of high purity cocaine concealed, which at that time had a street value of just over a quarter of a million pounds. It would have been nice if performance related pay had been based on a share of that… The gentleman was very co-operative in interview. He admitted he was really a Colombian national who had been recruited in Medellin. He was supplied with a Venezuelan passport in a false identity as he was told it would draw less attention than if he travelled on Colombian papers. He was to be paid 10,000 US dollars for his trouble, a tidy sum for him but a tiny fraction of the drugs' actual worth. As with so many couriers, financial hardship had motivated him; he was 15,000 dollars in debt, had alimony to pay for two children from a previous marriage and was also expecting a child with his second wife. This is not enough to excuse someone of a crime but I was sympathetic to most couriers like him. The real villains were the gangsters running the drugs trade who were the ones making the serious money and all too often not being brought to justice.

Life was slowly getting back into a routine for me. In the new year I took my children to a workshop day for bereaved children organised by St Barnabas. The idea was to help them come to terms with what had happened to them and to see that they weren't the only children to have lost a parent in tragic circumstances. The children were given activities to do and the adults were put into small groups to share their experiences. There I met Sallie who had lost her husband to kidney cancer and who had three daughters aged from six to nine. We got on very well and exchanged phone numbers but I thought no more about it until my regular visit from a St Barnabas counsellor some months later. I casually asked her how Sallie was doing to which she replied, 'Phone and ask her yourself.' I was reluctant as I certainly wasn't looking for a relationship and didn't want it to look like I was hitting on her. I finally plucked up the courage to ring and we chatted as comfortably as we did when we first met. A coffee was arranged a short while later and the rest as they say is history.

We married in 1999 having got a special licence to do it at St Barnabas. It was tough at first bringing up five kids but ultimately it has been wonderful for all of us. I've inherited another three lovely daughters, Harriet, Madeleine and Lydia, and Sallie and I are immensely proud of the young adults our five kids have become.

Once Sallie and I were together we shared childcare so it made it much easier for me to get back to working the full range of shifts. It was a while, though, before I got another drugs seizure but it was to prove the most interesting of my career for a number of reasons.

Chapter 22

MR AND MRS

It was a normal Sunday morning for me on duty in Gatwick's north terminal. The British Airways flight from Lagos had chocked, so I'd taken up my usual position behind the immigration desks waiting for the passengers to arrive. Once they did you'd move from desk to desk hoping to hear a story that would make you think 'potential drug smuggler'. I didn't have to wait long that morning as a Nigerian gentleman in his mid-40s explained the reasons for his trip. Once he'd had his passport stamped I started with a few questions of my own.

I first asked to see his ticket and was handed an old ticket with a transit leg on to Stuttgart that had been used some two months before. I asked him the purpose of his visit here but he said he was going on to Germany for a three-day visit to buy sports trophies. I told him he'd given me an old ticket and asked to see the ticket he was travelling on today. He somewhat reluctantly handed me a different ticket which not only showed his final destination was Gatwick but also told me he'd checked a bag in. I immediately asked him if he had baggage to collect here but he said no and said his bag was in transit to Germany.

My initial interest had already gone up several notches. His initial story to immigration was dodgy, he'd tried to palm me off with an old expired ticket and best of all he was trying to pretend his bag was in transit when it was clearly tagged to Gatwick.

As we went down to baggage reclaim the passenger nervously started pulling documents from his briefcase in an attempt to prove his business was genuine. I told him to wait to show me until we were in the customs hall, and asked him when he intended to travel on to Germany. He said he was going on by train tomorrow. When we got into the baggage hall I could see the Lagos bags were being delivered on belt 8 and asked him to retrieve his bag. He again said his bag was in transit to Stuttgart but I told him that was an impossibility if he wasn't flying directly on and that his baggage tag clearly showed his bag was to be collected here.

I directed him to belt 8, but he walked straight past it at some haste and stood next to belt 6. I escorted him back to the right belt and told him to pick up his bag but ten minutes or so went by with him making no attempt at all to identify his bag. By this stage my interest was going off the scale. It was clear from his behaviour that he had no intention of picking his bag up and the only explanation had to be that the bag was 'dirty'.

I informed a colleague what the tag number was and asked them to go to the rear of the belts to try and find it. He returned a minute later and pointed out a suitcase on the belt that our friend studiously ignored as it went past him. I finally lost patience, retrieved the bag myself and asked the passenger to accompany me to the customs hall so I could examine it.

As we approached the channels he ripped the baggage tag from the handle of the suitcase, whereupon a struggle for it ensued. Two or three colleagues joined the fracas but before we could rip it back from his grasp he managed to get it in his mouth and started to chew it. I knew it was breakfast time but a laminated baggage tag is not the most appetising fare. As none of us particularly wanted to get bitten we let him carry on with his meal.

I did, however, arrest and caution him on suspicion of importing a controlled drug, as three of my colleagues continued the struggle to handcuff him. His behaviour had given me reasonable grounds to suspect there were drugs in the bag before I'd even had a look.

Sure enough a short while later when we'd got our man into custody I found seven tape wrapped packages of cocaine concealed amongst foodstuffs in the bag. Our chap remained in an agitated state for a good while and continued to deny the bag was his. It took him the best part of an hour to finally chew down all of the baggage tag. In his subsequent interview he claimed the bag wasn't his and stuck to this story when he later pleaded not guilty at court. He said there was never a tag with his name on the bag and that Her Majesty's Customs had obviously tried to fit him up.

Unsurprisingly this didn't wash with the jury. We still had the reclaim tag on his ticket as physical evidence he'd checked a bag in as well as a statement from the airline. They also preferred to believe that our version of events was true. The judge wasn't that impressed, either, as he whacked him with a 12-and-a-half year prison sentence. It left him with plenty of time to chew over where he'd gone wrong.

A nice story in its own right but it didn't end there. Just over a year later I stopped a woman in the green channel coming in from Lagos who told me she was here to buy shoes and bags. Her back story fitted the usual profile so I decided to take a close look at the luggage amongst which was a soft-sided holdall with a very thick base. A probe revealed powder which reacted positively for opiates. We found a total of three packages in the false base; two contained heroin and one cocaine.

When she was in custody one of our investigators popped in for a look. He had searched an address in London in relation to my job from the previous year and said he recognised the woman as being there. It was then that we put two and two together and realised that they had the same surname. I had only managed to nick both husband and wife independently over a year apart. I'm not a mathematician but I imagine the odds on that happening would be pretty high.

The lady was equally as unforthcoming as her husband. When it was put to her that she was following his footsteps in the family business, she denied it and said her husband was safely tucked back at home in Nigeria taking care of the kids. She did follow his footsteps, though, in denying knowledge of the drugs and like him she pleaded not guilty at court. It didn't do her any good either, as the jury convicted her of drug smuggling. The judge in her case was marginally more sympathetic and gave her 11-and-a-half years inside. I guess he thought it would be nice for them to travel home together. They would certainly have plenty to catch up on.

Chapter 23

BOOTLEGGING, BACCY AND BLUE CHANNELS

The European Union has hardly been off the front pages in recent years, and the repercussions of the referendum and the decision to leave will no doubt rumble on for ages yet. The burning issues seem to be freedom of movement and immigration, but back at the turn of the century there was far more interest taken in the customs aspects.

When I'd started at Gatwick in 1985 the duty free allowances were straightforward and were the same wherever you came from. You were allowed one bottle and one carton and if you had more than that then the goods were liable to seizure. In 1992 though the waters were muddied by the introduction of the single market. Although I'm no expert in European law, this effectively set in stone the concept of free movement of goods within the EU as well as people. This had obvious consequences for Customs as this was at odds with imposing restrictions and allowances.

The answer was the introduction of the blue channel which was the new exit for any travellers arriving from within the EU. In theory we were not entitled to stop anybody in 'free movement', but the department were not stupid enough to let this risk go unchecked. We were therefore allowed to 'risk profile' any arriving passengers and still carry out checks. The risks were pretty obvious in the airport environment as EU and non-EU arrivals were mixing freely. It was not so straightforward at the ferry ports, though, whose only arrivals were from the EU, particularly the 'booze cruises' from France. The single market was hailed as a great thing for business and enterprise. It certainly attracted the enterprising minds of the criminal fraternity who saw it as a great opportunity to bring huge quantities of cheap booze and fags back from the continent to sell at vast profit.

Customs had to nip this sort of free movement in the bud as the loss to the exchequer of the revenue raised on UK alcohol and tobacco would have been catastrophic. Therefore 'free movement' was restricted only to goods for personal use. This was a grey area at the time and much legal argument was had over the ensuing years. The problems were becoming huge at the ferry ports with gangs of smugglers arriving on every boat. To try to arrest the problem, Customs exercised the law that entitled us to seize the means of concealment as well as the goods, which meant we began seizing the vehicles carrying the contraband as well. This 'war' carried on for many years and we experienced much the same thing at the airport, albeit on a much smaller scale. Clearly you could bring much more back in a van or car, but this didn't preclude gangs trying their luck by air.

For a long spell we had lots of people trying to bring bagfuls of cigarettes and tobacco through. There were many 'shit or bust' attempts made where there was no effort to conceal cigarettes, just a desire to cram as many cartons in a case as possible. With soft-sided suitcases it would often be possible to feel them with a simple pat of the outside of the bag. To aid the process of deciding what was considered 'personal use' the department published indicative limits. To begin with this was set at 16 cartons, 3,200 cigarettes. Although the Canary Islands are Spanish they are not considered part of the EU for tax purposes so the limit from there is still only one carton. Many a passenger would bring back their 'personal use' 16 cartons from there and express horror when we seized their goods. Call me a cynic but in most cases I'm sure they knew what they were doing, so any sympathy was in short supply.

Because cigarettes and tobacco are so cheap in the tax free Canaries, flights from there were often our best source of seizures. Mainland Spain also was producing although from there we had to resolve the issue of what was 'personal use'. On most occasions the obvious bootleggers were carrying so much that they knew it was futile to stay and argue the toss. I had one chap on a Malaga flight with two of the biggest suitcases I'd ever seen. It turned out he'd only been out for the day and had 44 kilos of hand rolling tobacco with him. I offered him the opportunity to stay and discuss whether they were for personal use but he barely paused to say goodbye. He did say something although I don't think it was anything too complimentary. Over the years I copped a fair amount of abuse from aggrieved punters. I never took it personally as it happened to pretty much any customs officer going about their business. We were hardly entrants in a popularity contest so any verbal was like water off a duck's back to me. You needed a thick skin and a technique for placating an angry passenger which I developed quite successfully over the years. There was no harm in empathising with a passenger as you seized their goods, and as long as their anger didn't escalate into a risk to my 'film star' good looks it was just part and parcel of the job.

Although drugs were still our prime target, the industrial scale of bootlegging in those days made that a very important issue. The single market was far from the only motive for tobacco smuggling as seizures were plentiful from all corners of the globe. The blue channel never developed into a free pass for passengers and in my experience the great British public never seemed to take too much of a shine to it anyway. I saw much head scratching over the years as to what it was for and most traditionalists plumped for the green channel anyway. If it is removed once we leave the EU, I can't see too many tears being shed for its loss.

My wedding day with Sharon – 16th September 1989. A perfect day – even Fulham managed a victory.

Marriage to Sallie in June 1999 at St Barnabas Hospice in Worthing, the place that had brought us together.

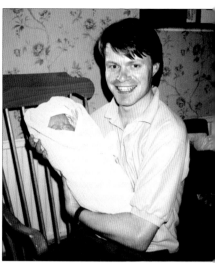

Top left: telling my son Daniel about my day at work. Gripped he wasn't.

Top right: Bethany arrives in June 1993 – and the proud father is doing his best not to drop her.

Above: Sharon was a beautiful wife and a wonderful mother to our children; they were her absolute pride and joy.

Right: I've been so fortunate to find love again and inherit three more lovely daughters. This is the Brady Bunch on a family holiday in 2003.

Top: my cap band with the famous portcullis proudly on display.

The team group is Dave Sawdon's Green team soon after Gatwick's north terminal opened in 1988. Don't we look smart!

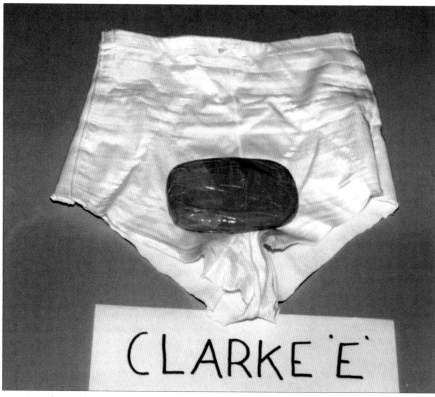

A package of cocaine found in the underpants of a gentleman we strip searched.

Packages retrieved from a swallower after a visit to our throne room. The ruler (in inches) indicates their size – not an easy meal to digest…

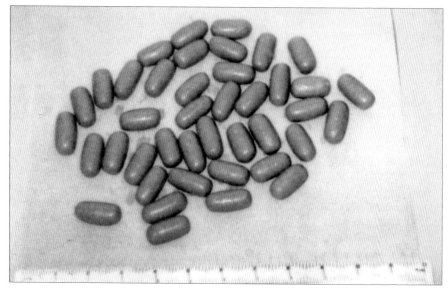

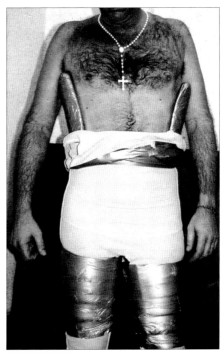

This chap was spotted walking rather stiffly through customs controls. A short while later a body search showed the reason why – multiple packages of cocaine taped around him.

A wheelchair passenger may have thought he was getting away with it. A search of his chair's tyres ensured he didn't.

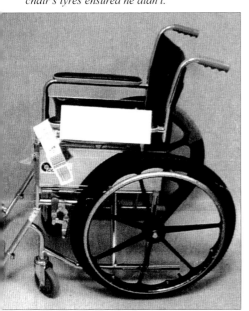
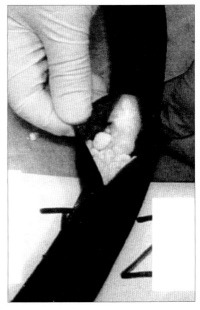

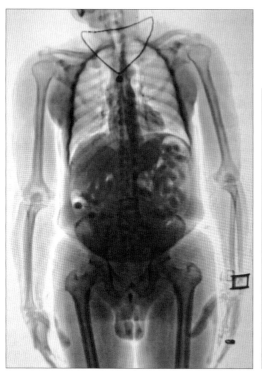

Top pictures: a body scan image revealing the tell-tale shape of swallowed packages – as the end product was to prove.

Above: These commercially sealed cans of foodstuff may have looked genuine, but judicious use of the airport's tin opener revealed the contents to be compressed cannabis.

Left: For a time, concealments in shoes were all the rage. Cocaine was hidden in this pair.

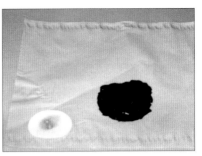

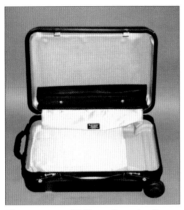

Top pictures: Hollowed-out heels were a popular hiding-place for drugs, often in the pair the courier was wearing, but also sometimes in extra pairs in luggage. The right-hand picture shows a white filter paper with a blue mark, the result of a drugs test that indicated the presence of cocaine.

Above: the classic hard-sided suitcase with a false bottom; this one concealed two kilos of cocaine, and was being carried by a Venezuelan chap I caught in late 1997.

Below: Ingenious concealments weren't only used for drugs. This is a box of chocolates I found on a Ukrainian woman; on closer inspection it contained a selection of cigarettes instead.

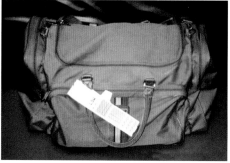

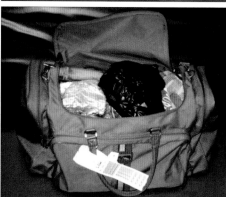

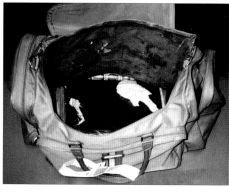

Left: a harmless camera bag carrying harmless bits and pieces – and cocaine hidden under a bottom panel.

Above: an elaborate concealment with strands of compressed herbal cannabis sewn into a handicraft raffia basket and table mats.

Below left: delicious sweets? Actually lumps of cocaine. The courier from Trinidad was carrying about one kilo of the drug, hidden in this way.

Below: bags containing dialysis solution for a kidney patient. Actually the brown liquid contained over ten kilos of pure cocaine.

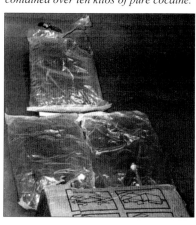

Chapter 24

THE NEW MILLENNIUM

Time flies when you're having fun is the old adage, and that was certainly the case for me with my job at Gatwick. When I was a kid I looked upon the year 2000 as some distant date in the future. I envisaged a space age society where we'd be driving around in flying cars and all our needs would be taken care of by robots. I couldn't imagine myself being 38 which was the age I attained that year. I thought if you were in your 30s you were middle-aged and anyone over 50 was essentially in God's waiting room.

By the time 2000 arrived I had spent 22 years in Customs, way over half of my lifetime at that stage, which was quite a sobering thought. I had also completed 15 years at Gatwick which hardly seemed possible. There had already been a few tinkerings within the organisation, but wholesale changes were still a little way over the horizon.

As the new millennium approached there were no signs of flying cars. The UK's cutting-edge idea for the new century was a glorified circus tent next to the River Thames. There was as much fear as excitement as doom-mongers suggested the millennium bug would cause all our computers to crash and trigger worldwide chaos. At Gatwick our biggest worry was that one of our bosses, who we were sure was using hair colourant, would find his Grecian 2000 had stopped working.

Although there was a lot of razzamatazz at the time, it was pretty much business as usual at the airport. Drugs jobs were still coming thick and fast. A colleague and I bagged a couple of young females coming back from Jamaica with 16 kilos of cannabis concealed in bammy cakes, a traditional dish whose main ingredient would usually be cassava. All sorts of foodstuff were used as concealments on Jamaican flights, but our staple diet was still swallowers. I was fortunate enough to intercept a carpenter allegedly here for a two-week holiday. Part of his downfall was that when we checked out his UK sponsor we found he had been involved in a previous drugs importation some seven years before. Our man certainly proved a chip off the old block as, after a positive urine test, he admitted to swallowing packages of coke.

By now we had more technology at our disposal in the form of what we called an ion track. These are smallish swabs that can be rubbed on items that will detect minute particles of given substances. They are now in common usage at airport security where they are looking for explosives. Our machines were set to test for illegal drugs and could assist in finding concealments in baggage as well as help indicate if someone had swallowed. Even if packages didn't leak they were often contaminated on the outside by the people handling and preparing them. This mild contamination would not put the courier at risk but there would be enough absorbed into their body to give a positive urine test or ion track. Our best approach would be to swab the shoes the passenger had worn as even the most fragrant of us will have slightly sweaty feet after a long flight. Any drug absorbed would be dispelled in bodily fluid and a positive ion track received from a pair of shoes or socks would often be an indication that the person had drugs inside them.

My first find with the aid of this technology was a 30-year-old Jamaican lady whose shoe gave a positive reading for coke. When I arrested her she asked if she could be sent home, which was often the response of somebody who knew the game was up.

Once she knew this wasn't an option, at least not immediately anyway, she confessed to swallowing some sixty packages.

As time wore on, technology was used more and more to assist but I often felt it could be relied upon too much. With the experience I'd acquired I preferred to trust my instincts more when weighing a passenger up. It wasn't that I was a dinosaur, resistant to anything new, but using technology could turn an examination into too much of a scientific process rather than a human interaction where a good officer could almost smell something was amiss.

My next job didn't require any sophisticated help as a Nigerian lady had two brand new holdalls that were still unfeasibly heavy even when empty. Not only that but there was a strong smell of glue from the base of each bag. Nearly five kilos of cocaine was found in the false bottoms. In interview I did resist the temptation to suggest her smuggling attempt had come unstuck.

Now that interviews were tape recorded and normally conducted in the presence of a solicitor, you had to take a supremely professional approach. You talked tactics with your colleague, or jockey as they were known, before you went in, to check the points you needed to cover. However, in an attempt to entertain ourselves further we would often challenge ourselves to interject with a certain phrase, be it a song title or any other topical bon mot. I presume most of the regular duty solicitors were aware of this predilection but as long as we didn't overdo things it didn't compromise proceedings. Heineken Schmeineken was the catchphrase of a certain TV lager advert back in the day and I do recall asking my old friend the venerable Geoff Williams whether he could slip this into one of his interviews. I thought it might prove tricky but Geoff was always on top of the game. As the smuggler gave another dubious answer Geoff exclaimed in incredulous tones, 'Heineken Schmeineken, you don't expect me to believe that, do you!!' I somehow managed to suppress my mirth and instead appreciated being in the company of a master. I often wondered if any juries reading transcripts of interviews in those days were in on it as well; I can't imagine Customs had the monopoly on this particular brand of humour!

John Whyte
Regional Head London and National Detection Region
Custom House, Nettleton Road
Hounslow, Middlesex TW6 2LA
Tel: 020 8910 3604 Fax: 020 8910 3616
john.whyte@hmce.gsi.gov.uk

HM Customs and Excise
Law Enforcement

John Clark
Gatwick Airport

7th November 2003

Dear John.

I would like to take this opportunity to congratulate you on achieving over 25 years service with H. M. Customs and Excise, and to thank you for your commitment to the Department during that time.

I am sure that during your career you have experienced many changes within the Department and the work we do. I hope that you have found it both rewarding and challenging and that you are looking forward to the rest of your career with Customs.

Yours sincerely

John Whyte

My letter congratulating me on 25 years service. You'd think that after such a long time they could've spelt my name right.

Chapter 25

FOOD FOR THOUGHT

Although drugs and revenue goods were our priority, there were many other prohibitions and restrictions to enforce. Importing meat in personal baggage from outside the European Union was always prohibited, but in my early days at the airport the issue wasn't taken that seriously. There was a certain lack of kudos in getting a meat seizure while much more interesting stuff was wandering past. There were so few meat seizures being made early in my career at Gatwick that a senior manager sent a notice on the issue demanding we up our game. Within a day a colleague who possibly wasn't taking the instruction to heart seized the ham from a sandwich that was the remains of a passenger's in-flight meal. Not only that he also seized the two slices of bread in question as he rightly pointed out they were the means of concealment. The manager in question who had a notoriously short fuse went ballistic when he found out. Funnily enough, as a result the sandwich seizure trend quickly died out.

We were, however, making a lot of bushmeat seizures from West African flights for which there was a thriving market from the diaspora here. It was common to find an animal known as grasscutter on Nigerian flights which was local terminology for the giant cane rat. Sadly we also sometimes found monkey meat. There was not only potential disease from this kind of thing getting into the food chain but there were also conservation issues. As time went on, public health concerns came into much sharper focus as several different problems came to light. BSE, or 'mad cow disease' as it was more commonly known, raised awareness, and later when foot and mouth broke out it was clear the department needed to be more proactive in its approach. For a time we had roving specialist meat teams whose sole priority was to seize prohibited foodstuff. Over the years seizures of POAO (products of animal origin) rocketed at Gatwick as it was obviously a serious problem. This didn't mean there was no room for humour, though.

When avian flu broke out there was a sense of panic amongst the top brass. We were told to take a zero tolerance approach on flights from risk areas. My line manager had us investigating a holiday flight from Turkey and said we should be checking clothing in case any items had contaminated bird poo on. I didn't quite go that far but did seize two boiled eggs from a couple who had taken them from their hotel breakfast table that morning. It wasn't my proudest moment and I'm sure we weren't making the difference in terms of stopping the virus reaching the UK. I may have been wrong but I always thought birds were freely flying across our coastline without making themselves known to HM Customs. Anyway we were secure in the knowledge that we'd done our bit, and to be fair bird flu never did take off. Swine flu was the next big thing and our response this time was to print thousands of public notices for concerned passengers to read. Uptake wasn't high, which meant we were left with boxloads to store. As with bird flu the swine flu scare pretty much came to nothing. After all pigs were never likely to fly.

As I say, conservation was also a big concern. The UK were signatories to the Convention on International Trade in Endangered Species (CITES), which meant we were on the lookout for things like crocodile skins and ivory as well as some traditional Chinese medicines which contained animal products. It was worthy work that possibly wasn't prioritised as highly as it should have been, although we did have our share of seizures at Gatwick. I recall a colleague heard some strange noises from a case during a covert bag examination at the back of the belts on a flight from the Far East. When he opened the bag he found about twenty small birds, most of whom had died on the trip. The unscrupulous offender was arrested and confessed how valuable these rare birds would have been to collectors here. The profits he hoped to make had helped him overcome any qualms about the cruelty he was inflicting. In many ways this trade was as reprehensible as the drugs trade where at least human 'victims' had an element of choice.

I had a couple of seizures of live animals myself, one by accident and one by design. In 2003 we'd received an anonymous tip-off that a man would be smuggling live tortoises back from Tunisia. Sure enough when I stopped him he had four baby tortoises in a cardboard shoe box in his hand luggage. Fortunately the creatures had survived the ordeal and were safely delivered to the animal welfare staff at the freight sheds. The elderly gentleman, and I use the term loosely, was arrested and was utterly blasé about what he'd done. Further investigation revealed he had been advertising tortoises for sale in his local paper and it was clear they fetched quite a tidy price. His greed outweighed any concern for the tortoises' right to live in their natural habitat. What was even more galling was that our CITES team couldn't pursue a prosecution because the particular species he'd brought in weren't on the endangered list. I was disappointed because this chap was well educated and well off and utterly arrogant about what he'd done. Give me a good honest drugs courier any day.

My other live animal seizure quite literally jumped out at me when I was searching a suitcase on a Jamaican flight one morning. As I pushed some clothing aside a frog hopped out and it wasn't exactly a baby either. I think I jumped quite a bit higher than the animal in question but with the help of a colleague managed to secure it in a suitable container. The passenger was equally as surprised as me to see it but said they were quite common in the area he'd been staying in Jamaica and it had obviously just decided to jump in his bag before he'd shut it for the flight home. The fact that it wasn't secured lent credence to the fact it was there by accident rather than design. As there was no question of an arrest in this case it wasn't long before I told the passenger to hop it. I later found out that it wasn't a frog but a cane toad which apparently has poisonous glands. If I'd known that at the time I'd have probably jumped higher still.

The frog incident was a good reminder not to be too casual when examining bags. It was good practice to only examine what you could see rather than blindly rooting round with your hands in a stranger's luggage. As you can imagine you never knew what you might come across and over the years I saw some items that would truly make your eyes water. Health and safety was drummed into us although we didn't always put it into practice. I saw many an officer get a nasty cut, although a lot of these were self inflicted with their own knives when sealing up seized goods. The knife was used to make a hole in the polythene bag for the plastic seal to go through and had a tendency to slip if you weren't careful. I managed not to injure myself in this way, and preferred this method to how we sealed goods when I started at the airport. In those days you were issued with your own individual customs seal with an embossed crown and a unique number. You then tied and knotted the seizure bag though a piece of cardboard over which you dripped hot wax. You then applied your seal before the wax set. It was a fiddly job that often left me with singed fingers whilst the older lags looked on with amusement. I probably wasn't as careful as I should have been over my time at Gatwick but I was quite fastidious about washing my hands after dealing with a grotty bag which held me in good stead. My health and safety light approach was probably shaped by the first training course I received on the subject. It was delivered by the designated H and S officer for the airport in a monotone and boring fashion. A few weeks later the very same chap broke his arm by falling out of an aircraft he had boarded when the steps hadn't been properly secured. For some reason we all found the irony in this a good deal more amusing than his training courses.

Chapter 26

VARIETY IS THE SPICE OF LIFE

Products of animal origin, be they live or dead, weren't our only source of unusual seizures. Life at the airport was never dull and with people arriving from every corner of the globe there were always interesting things to be found. Offensive weapons were prohibited and early in my career at Gatwick we were regularly finding flick-knives and the like. Typically they were carried by youngish men who were probably aspiring football hooligans rather than hardcore criminals. If it was just a single item rather than a cache of weapons we restricted our action to seizure and a warning. As time and technology moved on, though, we were finding more sophisticated items like stun guns or CS gas canisters. These we dealt with more seriously, normally by way of arrest and a trip to the custody suite. On one occasion in north terminal, a colleague found a suspicious package on a Venezuelan arriving from Bogota which turned out to be a live grenade. I shudder to think how the passenger got on a plane with it. Luckily it seemed the passenger was an oddball rather than a committed terrorist but the incident caused a lockdown and a good deal of consternation.

Over the years security became a much bigger issue, as airports and air travel were obvious targets. Back in 1985 you could access the 'airside' part of the airport purely on production of your departmental ID, but often security staff who knew you well would not even demand to see this. It was similar in immigration in those days, when officers had the autonomy to wave passengers past with just a cursory glance at the passport. From memory I recall Lockerbie being a big game-changer in terms of approach. Complacency was eradicated and all airport staff got machine readable IDs which had to be produced. My dearly departed colleague Keith Tatler was not keen on this new form of authority. Arriving at work one morning the security man barked, 'Pass' at Tatty as he strolled in. Keith nonchalantly replied, 'Thanks very much' and carried on walking.

Some old traditionalists resented the fact that customs officers should undergo screening but I considered it fair enough that we weren't considered special in that respect. The biggest disappointment for me was when the restrictions on liquids were brought in which stopped us bringing milk in from home for our early morning cuppa. Fortunately we were able to buy milk airside. After all no terrorist was going to come between a customs officer and their cup of tea.

Apart from offensive weapons there were numerous seizures of counterfeit goods. We didn't mind passengers carrying the odd fake watch or T-shirt, but if it was on a commercial scale we had a duty to the legitimate industry to take it seriously. Trading Standards were also interested if we found indications that shops were being sourced in this way and customers were being duped as to the veracity of what they were buying. All popular items were at risk of being counterfeited, and when viagra came on the scene we were making a lot of seizures of fake pills, particularly on flights from Goa in India. It was fairly small scale stuff and didn't really involve hardened criminals (pun very much intended).

Another common type of seizure was unlicensed skin lightening products. These were particularly popular with some Afro-Caribbean women. What most didn't realise was that a lot of these products contained dangerous carcinogenic extracts of mercury. A colleague was getting a lot of grief one morning from a woman who was quite irate that her lotions were being seized. I calmed her down by telling her that my colleague was only doing her job and pointed out the irony of me spending fortunes on sunny holidays to get my skin darker, while she was squandering her cash in an effort to look paler. It lightened the mood (pun again intended) and highlighted the fact, there's 'nowt as queer as folk.'

Anybody who's watched the Australian version of 'Nothing to Declare' will know how strict their customs are on what's coming in. Consequently their citizens were always concerned they weren't transgressing when visiting the UK and often asked us whether certain items they were carrying were alright. One morning a young Aussie declared to me a souvenir he was bringing as a gift here. 'What is it?' I asked. The chap seemed to forget what it was and after some hesitation finally told me it was a boomerang. 'I knew it would come back to you,' said I with the straightest face. I always liked a laugh and a joke with passengers when possible, and I was particularly proud of that one.

Until the laws on pornography were changed we were also making lots of seizures of video tapes. Laws in some other parts of the EU were more relaxed and it seemed incongruous seizing a film that had been bought legitimately in another member country. I recall a colleague seizing a tape that had actually been bought in an airport shop at Schipol in Amsterdam. I'm sure in these circumstances anyone taking their case to the European Courts would have got their films back. I'm not sure there was ever a test case though; perhaps people were too embarrassed to make their interest public. The nastier end of the market was something we took very seriously though. We were very much on the lookout for sex tourists returning from their sordid trips abroad and over the years many were encountered. Most were too shrewd to have anything illegal in their possession, although it didn't prevent us passing on valuable intelligence to other law enforcement bodies. To me this sort of criminal activity was equally as abhorrent as the drugs trade.

Chapter 27

MOVING ON TO DELTA ONE

Although it was always interesting getting involved in different work, nothing beat the buzz of getting a good 'cold pull' drugs job. However, by the early 'noughties' they weren't coming as thick and fast as they had previously. Maybe we were victims of our own success. It surprised me a little that drugs would come through our busiest airports where there was a good chance of encountering a customs officer. There were weaker chinks in our armour without doubt. Presumably drug gangs knew their quickest and cheapest way to top up supply was to stick a courier on a direct flight from a source country.

There was also obviously a limit to the amount of drugs an air passenger could carry. Far bigger consignments could be smuggled in by car, boat or by freight in container lorries. I never worked at a sea port but I was in awe of some of the concealments my colleagues there found. In some cases it truly was like looking for the proverbial needle in the haystack. I was as fascinated as anybody watching fly on the wall TV of some examinations. The thrill of making a find when you've stripped down a car or done a deep rummage of the nooks and crannies of a vessel must take some beating.

As our success started to dwindle, the first hints of wholesale reorganisation were seen. Permanent presence was withdrawn from smaller ports and airports where results weren't on the face of it so strong. As I said earlier, our preventive effect could not be measured statistically. Mobile teams were set up to react dynamically to risk and intelligence which meant that in theory these smaller places were still covered. The trouble with the target culture that had built up was that everybody knew they were measured by the amount of seizures made. Hence the 'mobiles' often turned up at the busier places like Gatwick where there were guaranteed richer pickings rather than cover risk at a less busy place. You could see why they did it. They had already lost their permanent posts at their home ports and obviously wanted to protect the job they had left. Unsurprisingly a lot of our staff resented their presence, especially if they picked up a big seizure we felt should have been ours.

Therefore the recent controversy about the risk to border controls with the advent of people smuggling is nothing new. It's impossible to cover every small port and airstrip 100% of the time. With 7,723 miles of coastline to cover, there is a limit to what can be achieved with finite resources. Intelligence is of course paramount but I fear we've lost the value of that acquired through the experience of 'local' staff. In any event all of this moving and shaking was far above my pay grade to worry about. Like most organisations, though, there was some resistance to change. The old joke asked, 'How many customs officers does it take to change a light bulb?' The answer was twenty. One to change it and 19 to say how good the old light bulb was.

These winds of change affected me personally when the team I was working on was disbanded. A senior manager was 'straw polling' us one day about how we thought things were going. Years of experience had taught me to keep my counsel in these circumstances. However, a younger tyro gave him chapter and verse on all that was wrong with the world. Unfortunately he chose to do it to the wrong person. The manager 'put the matter on paper' and suggested his insubordination was down to poor training and management. Our team leader, who was very able and a lovely bloke to boot, therefore took the lion's share of the blame. He was moved on and the team members were cast far and wide across the airport. As it turned out it was a lucky move for me. I ended up on Delta One under the command of the very experienced Jim Flockhart. I was to spend the next 12 years of my career there working with some super people.

Through all this upheaval the one constant was the adrenalin you got from a good old-fashioned drugs seizure. All of us went through dry spells where you wondered if you'd lost your touch. Seizures in general were harder to come by so these dry spells seemed to be getting longer and longer. The larger the gap between jobs probably heightened the buzz of the next one as it reassured you that you hadn't lost it after all. My first drugs job on Delta One was a very satisfying one as it wasn't off a traditional direct flight from a source country.

It was a Sunday lunchtime British Airways flight from Amsterdam where most of the clientele were Brits returning from a short weekend break. I stopped a woman who produced her British passport and said she'd been in Holland for a week visiting a friend. As the lady was of Nigerian origin I made the point of asking if she had travelled anywhere other than Holland to which she said no. There were no incriminating stamps in her British passport to suggest she was lying but to me she didn't feel quite right. Sure enough in her handbag was a Nigerian passport in her name; the woman had dual nationality. The stamps in this showed me she'd lied about spending a week in Holland but had merely transited through there for a trip to Nigeria. There was obviously no law against travelling to Nigeria so there could be only one reason why she'd pretended not to have been there. This was the stage where the hairs on the back of your neck stood up and you had to control your excitement. You knew you were on to something but you still had to be calm and methodical to make sure you didn't miss anything. In this case I didn't have to worry too much. The handbag the Nigerian passport had emerged from was soon empty but still weighed over two kilos. Packages of cocaine had been sewn into either side of the bag and there were more packages to be found in her suitcase. Her efforts to disguise where she'd been had proved fruitless and I'd picked up a seizure with a street value of some £275,000. A very tidy day's work for me and ultimately a very long 12 years inside for the lady to reflect where she'd gone wrong.

Chapter 28

TEAMWORK

Although the seeds of change were already being sown, and would later pick up pace, the one thing you could rely on in Customs was the support of your colleagues. I was fortunate enough to work with many fantastic men and women over the years, not only within my own teams but airport wide. On my return to work after the death of my first wife I was staggered to be presented with a cheque from my boss for £1,000. He said a collection had been made to raise funds to help me with my children, and people from all across the airport had been eager to contribute. I shouldn't have been that surprised really. Many of my fellow officers had attended Sharon's funeral and Customs was renowned for looking after their own when the chips were down. It wasn't only this financial help but the generosity of spirit when I came back to work that helped me through.

Teams typically had anything up to twelve people on if they were up to complement and you spent all your working life in the company of these same people. It's a cliché to say we were like family but in a sense it was certainly true. One could argue that any job is the same when you consider the time spent at work but the spirit engendered when working the anti-social shift pattern we followed was heightened. This camaraderie was vital as you were often in stressful or potentially violent situations where it was essential you knew your colleagues had your back covered. We were trained in arrest and restraint techniques which later became known as officer safety training. However, with a particularly violent or volatile offender, it often came down to sheer weight of numbers on your side to subdue them. Therefore it was reassuring to work in a team that stuck together whatever the circumstances.

Team spirit was fostered further by a fair amount of socialising out of work. As I alluded to earlier, 'old school' Customs had a fairly big drinking culture both within and out of work. Alcohol consumption on the job was eradicated completely long before the new millennium dawned but the traditions of the service were maintained by way of Christmas parties and team outings. As time went by and with the advent of budget airlines, outings became more sophisticated with many airport teams having a one- or two-night 'jolly' on the continent. Delta One put Milan, Palma, Prague, Alicante, Krakow and Valencia on its rich and varied CV, although it's fair to say that the choice of venues was pretty much where the sophistication ran out.

Our trip to Valencia coincided with the worst storm the city had seen in some fifty years. We'd ventured into the city that evening and dived for cover in the first bar we found as the heavens opened. 'It's just a passing shower,' said one of our number but unfortunately his weather forecasting skills weren't the equal of his ability to put a pint away.

Some four hours later we were still there as the monsoon had properly set in. The more sensible team members had jumped in cabs earlier in the night to find a restaurant or to get back to the hotel. However, yours truly and the hard core had remained in the same bar secure in the knowledge that the rain was about to ease up. Our luck was about to run out though when the staff told us it was closing time and bid us 'adios'. We asked if they could call us a cab but to be fair with most of the city's roads flooded there was more chance of a ride home on Shergar. In all honesty when we looked outside we'd have been better off asking if Noah and his ark were in town. We therefore ventured into the deluge on foot but this is where our trouble magnified.

As we'd cabbed it into town, none of us had a clue where our hotel was. The fact that not so much as a bag of crisps had passed our lips while we'd quaffed an industrial quantity of Valencia's finest ale also did nothing for our geographical ability. The term 'sat nav' has come into common parlance but in our situation it was more a case of 'twat nav' as we stumbled blindly on. Within a short time we were all frozen and soaked to the skin and our impromptu walking tour of the city wasn't looking such a bright idea. There were no taxis anywhere to be seen but we did hail a police car in the hope they might offer us directions. The language barrier meant that this idea didn't work out as planned. By this stage we were even hopeful they might arrest us, as a night in a warm and dry police cell looked pretty appealing.

Fortunately our luck was about to change when we recognised a landmark we'd seen earlier and a short time later we made it back to the hotel. My fun didn't quite end there as when I tried the key to my ground floor room it didn't work. I knew I was pissed but I was sure I had the right room. When I got back to reception I was told all my belongings were now in a room on the second floor as my room had been flooded. Passing shower it most assuredly wasn't. These trips were always good for team bonding and helped ensure you were a tight-knit unit within work too. Perhaps in hindsight the department should have funded them…

Although their financial generosity was never likely to stretch that far, the Civil Service used to heartily encourage participation in sport. Official time off was given for deserving causes as long as it didn't infringe on work, and I had the very good fortune to be a regular in the Gatwick Customs football side. We played in a Wednesday afternoon airport league and enjoyed a fair degree of success over the years. Other teams participating included Immigration, Gatwick Police, British Caledonian, British Airways and a few of the handling agents' firms. Their line-ups typically included a few burly loaders who weren't exactly fans of Her Majesty's Customs. Our work at the airport often interfered with any nefarious activity going on, so the opportunity to dish a little out in return on the football pitch wasn't going to be wasted. We could look after ourselves but I had the unfortunate reputation for getting injured, mainly because I was neither nimble or quick enough to avoid the rough stuff. These limitations were covered up in my regular position of full back where I put my twin assets of no height and no pace to optimum use.

Our line-up came from staff all across the airport, so the team spirit we built up on the pitch helped us in work too if we needed each other's assistance. It also helped keep us fit although the annual trip to the Channel Islands to play Guernsey Customs was only beneficial for the building up of your drinking arm. I only managed to go once as by the late 80s the practice died out. It was probably just as well as I'm not sure my liver could have taken many of these expeditions. On the occasion I went, we flew over on a Wednesday morning and played the match as soon as we got there in order to then concentrate on the main mission.

There were as many non-players as players in the party and they were imbibing freely during the match. As we didn't want to be left out we cracked open a few tinnies at half-time which probably helped explain why we drew 3-3 having led 3-1 at the break – that and the frequent stops for treatment when our 'physio' brought on the medical bag with a bottle of whisky purchased at the duty free that morning. Two nights enjoying Guernsey's finest hospitality then ensued before flying back after a lunchtime session on the Friday. We couldn't be accused of lacking stamina.

As 'austerity Britain' took hold pretty much all time off for sports and social events dried up. I guess that's fair enough in the current climate and by then my creaking bones had seen me hang my boots up anyway. I guess Gareth Southgate's England revolution will have to do without me.

Chapter 29

NEW HORIZONS

As the European Union expanded rapidly in the new millennium so did our opportunities to make seizures from different sources. Cigarettes were much cheaper in Eastern Europe as their tax rates were a lot lower than the UK. As new countries joined the EU we had more and more flights from the likes of Poland, the Czech Republic and the Baltic States. For an initial period the allowances from these 'accession' states were still restricted until their tax rates came more into line with the rest of the EU. Consequently we had a lot of success from these destinations. It wasn't quite on the scale of the bootlegging we had seen earlier but it certainly provided a boost to our figures. The break-up of the old Soviet Union and the fall of the Iron Curtain had also helped in this respect, as we were now getting regular flights from places like Belarus, Ukraine and Albania. The fact that these countries weren't in the EU also meant that animal products from these places were prohibited. On many occasions it was possible to seize a full set of meat, cheese, booze and baccy from one passenger which would considerably lighten their load on their onward journey. Strangely I don't recall anyone ever being grateful for this kind of assistance.

Gatwick has recently been in competition with Heathrow for an extra runway and has always tried to expand by taking in new airlines and routes. Any fresh flight got our attention until we could assess what risk it posed. For a time Vietnam Airlines ran regular scheduled services into Gatwick which provided a rich and plentiful source of business for us. Chicken feet are particularly popular in Vietnam and we found many of these amongst other delicacies on a daily basis. The UK probably has one of the highest duty rates in the world for tobacco so pretty much any other country could be a source for cheap cigarettes. Vietnam was unsurprisingly no exception although I was slightly taken aback by one smuggler I caught.

Experience taught us that smugglers could come in all shapes and sizes but I'd never caught anyone quite this small before. Unaccompanied minors, or 'unmins' as we exotically called them, were children travelling alone. Airline representatives would escort them through the red channel and deliver them safely to a responsible adult waiting for them outside. One morning an eight-year-old boy was presented to me on a flight from Ho Chi Minh. He was a cheeky little Londoner who'd been in Vietnam for three weeks to stay with his grandparents. He had a trolley full of luggage which he said grandma had packed for him to take home for his parents. I asked him if he knew whether they'd put any cigarettes in the bags. He was reluctant to answer in the same way I was when the teacher at school was asking who the culprit was. I therefore examined the luggage to find some 12,000 cigarettes secreted here, there and everywhere. I asked the airline rep to go out and find the responsible adult and a short while later she returned with the boy and his mum. I gave mum a dressing down as I seized the fags and told her to tell off her parents too for using their grandson as a courier. In the meantime the young man was finding the whole caper extremely amusing which left me with a less than straight face as I tried to tell his mum off. I'd often heard the phrase 'It's good to start young' although I'm not sure it would have been that appropriate in this case.

The multicultural nature of our country has provoked demand for all sorts of products. We older customs officers were often accused of being resistant to change but in one sense we were constantly evolving, in respect of the contraband we were looking for. In my early days we were looking for watches, jewellery and other revenue seizures like golf clubs and video cameras. As this type of seizure dried up we diversified into other areas. The boom in shisha cafes in the UK meant a huge growth in demand for fruit tobacco. Gatwick had many flights from Dubai and other places in the Middle East like Iraq which proved a good source of supply and a lot of trade for us. The aroma of the different flavours was wonderful and was gratefully received by our lock-up staff who were more used to dealing with rotting meat and over-ripe cheese.

The staple diet of the discerning customs officer was still drugs, though, and I was grateful to be part of a triple-handed cocaine seizure my team picked up in March 2003.

We'd had intelligence that three women from the West Midlands had been to St Maarten for a week on a drugs run and although information didn't always come up trumps, this time it did. The source was quite solid and our interest was piqued further when the ladies came through immigration separately and made a conscious effort to disassociate from each other at the reclaim belt. It did them little good as we intercepted them all in the green channel and found each had a similar concealment of four kilos of coke. My next job was also on a flight from the Caribbean but this time the couriers made a point of coming through together. It was a young Italian couple ostensibly returning from a romantic break in St Lucia. It was going to prove the last holiday they spent together for quite some time as they had a total of twenty kilos of cocaine concealed in the very thick false bottoms of two hard-sided suitcases. My own version of 3-2-1 played out, as the next job I had was on a single female traveller coming up from South Africa with a kilo of coke secreted on her person.

I've often been asked by friends what makes us stop the people we do. They probably thought I was being disingenuous when I'd say I couldn't always put a finger on why. The three seizures referred to above help illustrate why that is the case. The three women split up and pretended to be alone, the Italians made a point of being the star-crossed romantic couple, while the single woman portrayed herself as a carefree backpacker on her travels. People would do anything to put you off the scent so you had to be open-minded to all possibilities. To be fair the three-hander was a result of intelligence, and later in my career a lot more stops were done as a result of information received. However, the vast majority of interceptions made were 'cold pulls' and were based on intuitive assessment and past experience. Having said that, most people I stopped were completely innocent and a swift chat would often leave me satisfied without necessarily examining the luggage. However, years of observation of human nature would often tell me that something wasn't quite right and lead me to take things further. Often a seizure resulted and, although there was good fortune in being in the right place at the right time, success wasn't completely dependent on luck. Well that's what I told my bosses anyway.

Chapter 30

WINDS OF CHANGE

The saying goes that nostalgia isn't what it used to be, and there is a tendency to look back at past events with rose-tinted spectacles. As you've probably gathered, I thoroughly enjoyed my time as a customs officer. I joined when it was still Her Majesty's Customs and Excise and there was a sense of pride that you were part of a department with a long history and sense of tradition. However in April 2005 HM C & E was no more, as after the merger with the Inland Revenue we became HM Revenue and Customs. I could understand some of the logic involved as to a certain extent there was some duplication of function in terms of collecting revenue. However from a customs detection officer's perspective the change had no real effect and for a time it was business as usual at the airport.

To prove the point I caught a Nigerian swallower in May 2005 who fitted the time-honoured profile. He claimed he was here for five days to buy car spare parts. He was staying in a London hotel and had a nice round figure of £1,000 in cash. The only difference was that he'd flown in from Benin via Tripoli in Libya but this didn't deter us from requesting a urine sample. The positive result preceded the production of 105 packages and a significant spell at Her Majesty's pleasure thereafter.

My next detection gave me a greater sense of pride as it fitted a distinctly different profile and was down to my alertness and powers of observation. Colleagues of mine would argue that I was hardly known for these qualities but in an effort to blow my own trumpet I will paint the picture. A lot of our time was spent at the entrance to the channels. Regular passengers may have often spotted a gaggle of officers positioned there and probably thought we were there just trading office gossip and watching the world go by. To a degree they would be right but we were always on the lookout for a 'decent bet' to intercept. The blue channel was only meant to be used by people arriving from EU countries. To assist us distinguish between EU and non-EU arrivals, baggage tags on EU flights had green edges to them. If a bag had originated on a flight from outside the EU, or had merely transited through, then it would have a plain white tag.

I was on duty early one afternoon and was aware the TAP flight from Lisbon was in the hall. The flight had good connections from South America, in particular Brazil, and had been the source of several cocaine seizures in the past. Consequently I was observing the Lisbon reclaim belt closely in the hope of spotting something interesting. I noticed a smartly dressed middle-aged man of Latin American appearance collect two pieces of luggage both with non-EU white baggage tags. The bags weren't in keeping with the man's business-like appearance and my interest was piqued further when he tried to make a quick dart down the blue EU channel. My instincts served me well as although the gentleman had an Italian passport this did not give him the right to use the blue channel. His flight had originated in Fortaleza, Brazil, and one of the two bags had a concealment of two kilos of cocaine. The chap had actually been born in Argentina and had managed to acquire a genuine Italian passport through ancestry. This had made him an ideal courier in the eyes of the gang that recruited him as they thought he'd draw less attention than someone on a South American passport. It's true that it abetted his passage through immigration but it did him no favours when I apprehended him in the customs hall. It served to demonstrate the subtle differences between immigration and customs work.

For sure the roles do have much in common but in my view it was good to have expertise in one role or the other.

It wasn't long though before the powers that be started to think differently. There had long been rumours of a Border Police force or something of that ilk, and in 2008 the UK Border Agency came into being. Tranches of our work remained under the remit of HMRC but customs at the border was merged with immigration under the umbrella of the UKBA. Initially we were told that specialisms would remain and we could still focus specifically on customs work. However as austerity took hold the mantra was 'more for less' and multi-functionalism took over. From the government's point of view it made sense if they could get two jobs done for the price of one, although as a 'dyed in the wool' customs man my opinion was somewhat different. It took me many years to acquire all the skills necessary to be a good customs officer and I'm sure those on immigration work would be of the same opinion. I'd often say that you wouldn't call in an electrician if your plumbing needed fixing. Even if I thought the quality of our work would be diluted by all the change, as a humble government servant it wasn't my place to say. Consequently we all adapted as best we could even though we were becoming a political football in the process. By 2013 we had been renamed again as the UK Border Force and as I write this remains the case. The government obviously has every right to organise the public services as it sees fit. It's just that the demise of HM Customs and Excise has given my tinted spectacles an even rosier hue.

Chapter 31

THE VIGILANT MOTHER

If asked I would always say the best aspect of being a customs officer was in making a good drugs detection, particularly if it was of your own making rather than as a result of information supplied. Although I ended up doing over 30 years in the front line at Gatwick the little buzz felt when you knew you were on to something never left me. As rewarding as drugs seizures were, possibly the most satisfying piece of work I ever did was as the result of the vigilance of a caring mother.

I was on duty in the north terminal one August afternoon in 2008 when a rather distressed woman approached me and told me that a male passenger had taken photos of her two young daughters whilst they had been waiting at the baggage reclaim belt. She said she'd challenged him and asked him to show her the pictures and delete them but that he'd refused her request.

I asked her to identify the man to me and she pointed out a smartly dressed man of about 60 waiting at belt 1 for luggage from the EasyJet Rome flight. I told her I would deal with the matter from there and took her details should we need to contact her further. I then waited for the man to get his bags and intercepted him as he entered the green channel. I established he was an American citizen who said he'd been to Italy on holiday and was over-nighting in the UK before flying home the next day. I then told him an allegation had been made about him taking photos in the baggage hall and asked to see his camera. He handed over his digital camera without protest but when I examined it found the memory card had been removed. I asked him where it was and told him that there was no point trying to conceal it as my search would go to any lengths necessary to find it. He then rather sheepishly produced the memory card from his trouser pocket.

I replaced the card in the camera and the first image I saw was of the lower half of a young girl's body. The girl was sitting astride a baggage trolley and her underwear was visible in the picture. It was clear to me that this could be no accident and that the picture must have been taken with this motive in mind. I examined the man's luggage and found four more memory cards. Furthermore, from looking at the stamps in his passport I could see he'd regularly visited known sex tourist destinations such as Cambodia, Thailand and Vietnam. In light of what had been found I detained his camera and memory cards and contacted the police who attended immediately and arrested him. They took a statement from me and from the mum who'd set the ball rolling and subsequently got admissions from the man in interview.

He pleaded guilty the next day to the taking and possession of indecent images and was given a large fine and placed on the sex offenders register. He was then immediately deported to the USA where the authorities were waiting to arrest him with a warrant to search his house, having been informed of his activities by the police here. I believe more unsavoury material was found there and further punishment ensued. All of this because of the actions of a watchful and determined mother.

Over my career at Gatwick we were always on the lookout for paedophiles returning from the more commonly known sex tourist destinations. Generally they were too shrewd to be carrying any material we could arrest them for, but we were often able to provide intelligence for other authorities to act upon. Having dealt with a few over my career, what made me shudder most was how calm, detached and guilt-free they seemed to be.

I understand this is a common trait. However, as much as they made your flesh crawl, it was important that you remained calm and professional in order not to jeopardise any possible case. To those law enforcement officers that have to deal with these sort of offenders full time, I salute you. Booze, baccy and drugs was much easier territory.

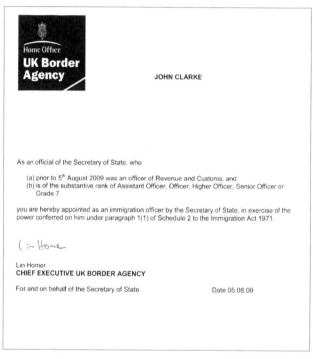

Appointed as an immigration officer, and thereby a certified Jack of all trades.

Chapter 32

WORK EXPERIENCE

It may be different now but when my kids were at school they had to arrange to do some work experience when they were in year 10. Consequently both my son Dan and daughter Beth had the dubious pleasure of accompanying me to work for a few shifts when they were 15. I recall one witty colleague tell Beth that he had never experienced seeing me do any work, so was at a loss as to what she was doing with me at the airport. Piss-taking was very much part of customs life and I thoroughly enjoyed both dishing it out and being the recipient.

To be fair they were pretty fortunate to do their work experience in a busy airport environment. It beat what many of their classmates had arranged and both of them were lucky enough to see me get a drugs seizure, although not as lucky as I was to have made them.

During their time there I tried to show them both a broad range of the work we did, and this included a trip to the custody suite where we had special toilets for the use of swallowers in our care. On Dan's visit I was demonstrating to him how we retrieved packages from the sealed unit when I happened across one that had somehow got lodged in the system. As there was nobody in custody at the time it was going to be nigh on impossible to tell who might have passed it so I had to put it down as an 'unowned' seizure. It was credited to my stats as a class A drugs detection but necessitated absolutely no paperwork or further effort on my part.

If this was a free gift, I surpassed that a few years later when I actually got a drugs seizure in my sleep. I was on my meal break in the south terminal rest room one evening having a power nap when I was rather rudely awoken. The chap explained he was an engineer who had been called out to do some maintenance on our special toilet and that he'd discovered something I might be interested in. He too had found a package lodged in the bowels of the unit and I was once again in receipt of an easy 'unowned' seizure. Incredulous colleagues couldn't believe my good fortune although I took delight in telling them with a wink that you made your own luck in this game.

Having said that I wasn't the first officer to get a drugs seizure in these circumstances. Many years earlier a colleague who was notorious for his ability to sleep on a washing line decided to get his head down in one of the cells on his meal break. His intention was to take advantage of the comfortable mattress provided but was perturbed when it felt lumpier than usual. It prompted a closer inspection which revealed a package of drugs that a canny smuggler had obviously secreted whilst there to be searched. It was a valuable reminder for us all to remain vigilant when we had somebody in the cells and to make sure we searched the room both before and after we took somebody in there. Although my colleague was disappointed not to get his nap, a nice unowned class A seizure was a good consolation. It's fair to say that over his career he did manage to catch up on his rest. In light of all this I did consider asking management if I could sleep for longer at work in the hope it would improve my detection rate. However, having slept on this idea I thought better of it.

Dan enjoyed his time with Delta One and particularly appreciated one incident. John Page was slightly older than me and was relatively new to customs work having spent most of his career in banking. Franco was at the other end of the age scale but had been on the team a little longer. What they had in common was that they both hailed from south-east London and were diehard Charlton fans. Despite this distinct lack of judgment on their part they were both very able when it came to the job. On one of Dan's shifts he saw JP and Franco enthusiastically get their teeth into a punter whose story was distinctly dubious. Ultimately I think they were satisfied and let the chap depart having given him their full repertoire. I explained to Dan that they had slightly amended the concept of the good cop, bad cop routine. What he had just witnessed was the modified bad cop and even worse cop version. I don't know if the experience had any lasting effect on Dan, although strangely enough he has never shown the slightest inclination to follow my career path.

Beth saw a more interesting seizure on my part as this time there was an offender involved. However, again the job rather fell into my lap as two police officers presented to me a man they'd arrested on his return from Jamaica. They explained that a warrant had been out for his arrest and asked if I would search his bags before they carted him off to the nick. His trip to the police station was delayed somewhat though as he'd concealed several packages of herbal cannabis in his suitcase. He therefore made the shorter trip to our custody suite first which gave Beth a first-hand insight into how we knocked off a drugs job. She thoroughly enjoyed her time at the airport but like Dan never expressed interest in pursuing it as a career. It looks like the family trade is dying out with me.

Chapter 33

NERVOUS BEHAVIOUR

Many people tell me they are always nervous when they come through customs. To be fair I don't blame passengers for being a little uncomfortable as they pass our gimlet-eyed stare. It is a little disconcerting knowing somebody is looking at you. If I'm on a train and I sense the person opposite is staring at me then it sets me on edge. Therefore it's quite normal to be tense in the customs controls; it was just part of our job to try and distinguish between natural and unnatural nerves.

A lot of different behaviours are on show in order to look relaxed but often they are so rehearsed they achieve the opposite effect. The advent of the mobile phone has had a massive effect on modern life and we saw more and more people on them as they came through customs. Often they'd be having inane conversations in order to show how unflustered they were. This was the case with a woman who entered the green channel one morning busy on her phone. The trouble was that I didn't think she looked relaxed at all and, what was more, there were notices up forbidding phones in the customs hall. My boss had a particular bugbear with people using their phones and was regularly threatening to confiscate them. I wasn't so bothered by her transgressing any regulations but more by the fact she just didn't look right.

My opening questions helped prove my hunch was correct. She said she was returning alone from a holiday in St Kitts having spent just a week there. I put it to her that it was unusual she'd gone all that way for such a short length of time. She replied she'd travelled out with friends who were staying there for longer but that she had to rush back for work. I asked what she did and she said she worked in a care home. This made me even more suspicious because as worthy as care work is I knew it wasn't the highest paid profession. Rightly or wrongly I didn't feel this woman was the type who could afford a week's holiday in the Caribbean and by now the relaxed demeanour she'd tried to demonstrate had disappeared completely.

My suspicions were proved right a short while later as I found a laptop bag in her case which was heavy enough to contain a computer but was empty. The reason for this was that a kilo of cocaine had been sewn into each side of the bag. I never did find out if the call she'd been on was stage managed to look nonchalant but if it was it didn't work.

I was quite chuffed with this job as by this stage in my career 'cold pull' detections were becoming fewer and farther between. The emphasis had switched to being intelligence led and although some success was achieved in this way it wasn't as satisfying as finding something solely because of your own intervention. As I stated earlier, other changes were picking up pace which again affected the ability to do more traditional customs work. In 2008 after the creation of the UK Border Agency I was formally trained to be an immigration officer. To begin with we weren't called into action very often but over a period of time this began to change.

In 2009, after a government bill received royal assent, I got a formal letter telling me I was now an immigration officer and a general customs official. Call me old-fashioned but it didn't quite have the same ring as the title customs officer. I knew that we had to adapt and as the saying goes no change is no option. However, it surprised me that there was such a rush to dispense with the past.

Over time the pace of change became more rapid. Jim Flockhart had by now retired and after 12 years on Delta One an internal reorganisation saw me jump up one letter and join Echo One. It was a great move for me as the boss was none other than my old friend Moaner, the very chap I'd done my initial training with in 1985. Although he took great delight in grumbling he was a very modern-thinking man. I was quite a senior citizen on a young and keen team but the change did me good and helped rekindle my enthusiasm. We had a lot of success and fun as a team but it wasn't to last long as another shake-up wasn't far round the corner. The powers that be decided we should have fewer but bigger teams and Echo One was collateral damage. My next team were fine but by now I was starting to tire of the constant upheaval and changing demands of the job.

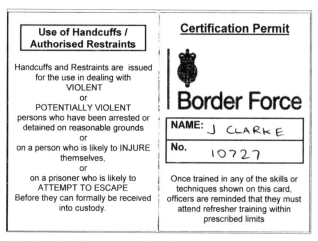

My handcuff permit that had to be renewed at refresher training each year. On role plays I was told I was technically proficient but not dynamic. People who know me may concur with that description, well, the second bit anyway.

Chapter 34

KEEPING CONTROL

A lot of people can get angry just being stopped by Customs, let alone having their bags searched or having goods confiscated. The trouble is that some take it personally rather than accept it as an occupational hazard of travelling. Security screening is accepted readily but everybody has to undergo that. I guess the difference with a customs officer stopping you is it can make you feel singled out. I can say hand on heart that it was never personal on my part. I was being paid to perform a job that was in theory protecting society.

We also had targets to achieve so I was hardly going to sit around all day twiddling my thumbs when I could be in the channels doing something interesting. I was always prepared to explain why I had stopped a passenger if they asked, although some individuals were so cross they weren't really interested in anything you had to say. All they saw was a uniform in front of them as they hurled a volley of abuse your way. That's why it was like water off a duck's back to me, as they had an issue with authority rather than me as a person. Sometimes passengers were prepared to listen and a well delivered put-down could restore some calm. Often though I'd just carry on with my job until eventually the anger subsided.

Thankfully the vast majority of people are compliant so I didn't encounter abuse too often over my career, although I would say in recent years it was becoming more frequent. I don't know if that's a sign that society is becoming less tolerant or me just not being able to remember too far back. As I say, verbal didn't bother me as it meant the person was getting rid of their pent-up frustration without resorting to physical violence. I was far more wary of a person whose anger was simmering just below the surface. The most menacing person I ever encountered was a guy returning from one of the Balkan states with six or seven cartons of cigarettes over his allowance. If looks could kill then I was very much a dead man and to look at him I was pretty sure he'd be able to achieve the feat with his bare hands. Colleagues were on hand had the situation escalated but I had the feeling he would probably have taken out the lot of us. It was very important not to show fear on duty as this would compromise your ability to control matters. How I managed it that day I'm not quite sure although he must have noticed the colour draining from my cheeks as I seized his fags. He tore the seizure paperwork from my hand and refused to sign it which on that occasion was absolutely fine by me. It was only halfway through my shift so I didn't think he'd be waiting outside for me when I finished, although it didn't stop me scanning the concourse a little more closely than usual that night.

If that was scary, sometimes I found the verbal insults very amusing. A colleague was seizing some fags on a Canary flight one evening off a bloke who was insisting that it was Spain and therefore part of the EU. I thought I'd be helpful and show him the public notice which clearly stated the Canaries were not considered part of the EU for Customs purposes. 'Who f***ing asked you? You're so f***ing ugly I bet you've never had a girlfriend,' was his opening gambit, as my intervention had only added fuel to his fire. His comments may have been fair in the sense I've got a good face for radio, so I didn't bother telling him I had a wife and five kids at home. To be honest he was that incandescent he wasn't in a listening frame of mind as my mate took 20 odd cartons off him. This was quite a few years back so

I hope the bloke has calmed down by now. We certainly had a good chuckle after he left that night as I told my mate I was just popping to the gents to crack the mirror.

When I started in the job we didn't have any formal arrest and restraint training so we had to rely on our instincts if ever things kicked off. Eventually the department realised that as a law enforcement body we needed to be taught some proper techniques. We therefore got a modified version of what the police were doing and over the years these courses have been developed and refined. Over my career I attended many refresher courses where you would re-visit and practise what you'd been taught. You had to pass each time in order to have your handcuff permit renewed and I'm pleased to say I stumbled through on every occasion. At the end of each course you received feedback from your trainers and a recurring theme for me was that while I was technically proficient I could do with being a little more dynamic. Although I probably shouldn't have been, I was quite proud of not being too dynamic! Perhaps I'll ask to have it put on my gravestone…

Chapter 35

THE BAD APPLE

Although I've referred often to the amount of fun and enjoyment the job has given me, I was always aware of the responsibility I had. Customs officers had extraordinary powers given to them which made us the envy of all other law enforcement bodies. Officers were issued with a beautiful commission produced on parchment style paper which explained our powers in quite flowery prose. Part of the wording read 'praying and requiring all and every constable and member of Her Majesty's armed forces or coastguard and all others whom it may concern to be aiding and assisting to him in all things'. What this effectively meant was we could direct anybody to assist us as we felt fit if the need arose, including members of the public. With powers that far-reaching we had to use them wisely, so it was very unlikely that we would need to use them in our day to day routine. I do recall an occasion when a member of the public interceded on our behalf without any bidding though.

A colleague had just arrested a drug smuggler in the green channel when he made a dash for freedom out of the exit on to the arrivals concourse. With various uniformed bodies in hot pursuit a helpful gentleman stuck out a leg as the guy ran past him and sent him sprawling. It would have undoubtedly been worth a yellow card on a football pitch but as it led to the swift re-capture of our man his intervention was very gratefully received.

In giving us these powers the department was also giving us a great deal of trust that we would use them judiciously and wisely. It was therefore one of the saddest moments of my career at Gatwick when a colleague breached that trust in the worst way imaginable. With hindsight it was possible to see it coming although it was also maybe part of the reason that he was ultimately caught.

It was probably around 2003 or 2004 that word spread amongst us that one of a colleague's detections had led to a very interesting interview with the smuggler he had caught. In it the guy had said that he should never have been apprehended as he was expecting to be met by a customs officer on his arrival who he was told would see him safely through. He wasn't able to name him but did say he'd been told he would spot him fairly easily as the officer would be wearing a uniform jacket. The full uniform back in those days was quite a thing of beauty and was not dissimilar to that worn by Royal Navy officers with gold braid on the sleeves of the jacket. However in an air-conditioned airport environment very few of us actually wore our jackets on duty. Their wear was generally saved for court appearances where we were expected to look our very smartest. I don't know whether this interview was the trigger of the intelligence but if it was it would have helped massively to narrow down who the officer might be.

From what I subsequently found out the prime suspect was put under surveillance and like many before and since did a pretty poor job of covering his tracks. He started arriving for work in a state of the art car which was hardly consistent with his salary as a humble public servant. In fact after his capture it came out in his trial that in the first six months of 2004, in addition to buying a BMW, £125,000 had gone into his wife's and his bank account. They had also bought an expensive new home, had five-star holidays in Barbados and Egypt and had bought a plot of land in the Caribbean for £40,000 with the intention of building a mansion there.

The scam had obviously been going on for some time and was quite simple in the way it was carried out. The bad apple fed the organisers details of his roster so that smugglers could be put on flights when he was on duty. In return he was given details of the couriers he would need to look out for and what flights they were on. He would then ensure he was close by as they entered the customs controls so he was able to effect an interception before anybody else. This put the couriers off limits to his honest colleagues and after a cursory chat from him and no examination of the luggage the smugglers were safely through with their contraband. As so often with criminals it was greed, as well as a great deal of good intelligence work, that gave him away and he was eventually apprehended after letting another couple through with bags full of cocaine that they had not even bothered to conceal. They had £2.4 million worth of the drug and were seen laughing on the concourse thinking they had successfully got through before being arrested. My colleague had also thought another successful mission had been accomplished until plain clothes investigation officers nicked him as he returned to our back office. The old adage that 'crime doesn't pay' was therefore proved true as ultimately his wife was successfully prosecuted on money laundering charges whilst my colleague got a 15-year sentence as much for the massive breach of trust as for the drug smuggling.

It was very sad for all of us that a guy that we'd all liked had let us down so badly. I'm sure he's had plenty of time since to reflect on the error of his ways.

Chapter 36

KEEP SMILING

Before I get too downbeat I'll try to lighten the mood. Those that know me would say I'm quite an easy-going bloke. It's a characteristic I inherited from my old man who loved the company of people and enjoyed life to the full. He sadly passed away in 2003 but his influence on me is still profound. At Gatwick I had the reputation of being something of a joker and many colleagues had the misfortune to hear my repertoire on more than one occasion. Humour was never far from the surface and I had the privilege to be in the company of many characters over the years, some of whom are sadly no longer with us.

There is a story about one dearly departed colleague that has become part of Gatwick folklore, and I feel it would be a shame not to share it. It was many years ago in the pre-PC days that this officer returned from a particularly hospitable meal break. Being a dedicated chap he went straight into the channels where he immediately stumbled over (not quite literally) a guy with a body belt of cannabis on a Malaga flight. It was a little while before the interview took place as the duty solicitor was called out. However, despite the ingestion of copious amounts of black coffee our hero was still not quite firing on all cylinders when he started to question the punter. He was clearly struggling for inspiration, so much so that the solicitor interjected fairly early in the piece. 'Officer, that's the third time you've asked my client the very same question.' The spontaneous response was classic: 'Yes, that's right, and I shall carry on asking that question until I can think of a different one.' Perry Mason it possibly wasn't, but it was pretty damn good in the circumstances.

Even though we were doing serious work it was always easier going about business with a smile on your face. Officiousness was not in my nature so I was always happy to inflict my brand of humour on passengers when I could. Mishandled bags are a common occurrence at airports. Unclaimed bags would be removed from the carousel and placed on the floor until a handling agent removed them. These bags had been security screened so weren't a risk but passengers would rightly report their concerns to you if they saw an unattended bag. I thanked and reassured them but normally followed up with the line 'If you see me running, try and keep up.' Not a classic I know, but it often provoked a smile although admittedly not too often with Americans. We share a common language but we are quite different breeds and irony isn't generally their strongest suit. A middle-aged American lady approached a colleague once and asked, 'Do you work here?' Although not as debonair as George Clooney, he was attired in the full customs uniform. He resisted the temptation to use one of my favourite lines, 'Not if I can help it', but instead replied, 'No, madam, I'm in fancy dress.' The woman looked nonplussed until her husband arrived on the scene and attempted to ask my colleague something. The woman swiftly interrupted him and said, 'Don't ask him, honey, he doesn't work here.'

Practical jokes were a bit of a feature too, although these were reserved for staff rather than the travelling public. We did have some standards after all. Although I'm now into my sixth decade my penchant for the juvenile has never quite left me. It's fairly common knowledge that the government regularly reviews the threat to national security, and notices were placed on the walls in our accommodation to signify the current level of risk. Therefore when a 'heightened' notice went up I couldn't resist the temptation to put a chair on a desk and replace it as high up the wall as possible. It triggered a fairly pompous email from management about taking the matter lightly and about health and safety concerns for the person who changed the notices over. It wasn't my intention to be flippant about security but the criticism was fair enough I suppose. Perhaps it's about time I grew up.

If I've given the impression that we were always clowning around, I apologise. Our work was a serious business and we were very much focussed when we needed to be. However, as in any job humour was a vital ingredient in keeping a happy and motivated workforce. The loss of my wife to cancer at such a young age only heightened my sense of perspective that life was to be enjoyed. I therefore knew how lucky I was to have been in a job that gave me such a lot of fun over the years.

A spell in charge. The date on the letter is obviously coincidental…

Chapter 37

THE FINAL FURLONG

As I've made pretty clear, I thoroughly enjoyed being a customs officer. When I joined HM Customs and Excise as a sixteen-year-old in 1978 I had no inkling what I really wanted to do with my life. I'd gone straight from school without really knowing anything about the department and all its traditions. I therefore went in blind, thinking that if I didn't like it I would rapidly move on and try something different. The fact that I was lucky enough to be posted to the Investigation Division was a huge sway in making me stay. The work was interesting from the off and the ready way I was accepted as part of a team made me feel pretty special. My next posting to the VAT Office wasn't quite as exciting, but it had been on promotion so the money I was making was very good for a young man still living at home. I spent three-and-a-half years there before the lure of Gatwick got to me. I was 22 when I transferred and little did I know then that was to be where I would spend the next 31 years of my career.

It took me a while to adjust to airport life and shift work but once I had my feet under the table I couldn't imagine working anywhere else. For sure, with shift pay and overtime, the money was pretty decent but that wasn't my prime motivation. I swiftly realised that catching smugglers was bloody good fun and as I developed my skills enough to start finding drugs on a regular basis I really loved the work. Ideally I'd have been good enough at football to play professionally and I'm sure notching the winning goal in a big match or performing on stage must trigger a huge adrenalin rush. Mere mortals like me have to get our kicks in a different way though. I guess for paramedics it would be the saving of a life or for a businessman it'd be the closing of a big deal. For a customs officer the biggest buzz you could get was from detecting a decent drugs job. There was no need to sample the stuff; the high came from finding it in the first place.

Gatwick was good to me in many other ways too. I was lucky enough to meet my first wife in the job and when she got ill I got all the support I could want from the management there. The warmth and friendship I got from colleagues after her tragic death was a massive help to me at a very dark time in my life. I will be forever grateful for this as well as for all the fun I had over the years.

Towards the end of my career drugs seizures were getting fewer and farther between but there was still a bit of life in the old dog. The last swallower I caught had a bit of a twist in that he was a Nigerian but had arrived not from West Africa but the Caribbean. He claimed he'd gone there to conclude a business deal but what gave him away was his paperwork. His briefcase was full of documents but there was nothing in there less than five years old. He was cordially invited to undergo a body scan which showed he was what we called in the trade PFOI (packed full of it). The Caribbean was also the source of the last two drugs jobs I got. One was a woman with a traditional concealment of cocaine in shoes but the other was a man with quite an innovative concealment in bottles. The top and the bottom of the bottles had liquid in them but the middle section which was hidden by the surrounding label was full of coke. I didn't know then that it would be the last drugs job I'd get but in hindsight it was quite a nice concealment to bow out on.

I was very lucky to have had the career I had, and I worked during the period when the so called 'war on drugs' was at its zenith. We were catching couriers galore in those days but towards the end of my time at the airport the focus had very much switched to immigration and border security. It's a sign of the times I guess. Hardly a day goes by now when there's not a story on a front page somewhere about the topic. Drugs don't seem to be the burning issue they were back in the 80s and 90s. As Customs was absorbed into the UK Border Agency and then the Border Force, priorities seemed to change rapidly. Consequently I wasn't enjoying the job as much and, after thirty odd years of shift work and a long commute to the airport, I thought it might be the right time to step aside. Fortunately I found myself a Monday to Friday job much closer to home and so in June 2016 I rode off into the sunset. I wasn't as emotional as I thought I'd be on my last shift. I can be a bit of a sentimental old fool so thought I might shed a few tears as I said my farewells. The fact I didn't confirmed to me it was the right time to go.

Just a few days later the country voted to leave the EU. The Brexit campaigners saw it as the way we could retake control of our borders. Having worked where I do I'm sure it's not going to be as simple as that. Mr Cameron took the coward's way out and stepped aside to let somebody else sort it all out, and as I write (March 2019) the whole saga still has a long way to run. It will undoubtedly have ramifications for the Border Force and the colleagues I've left behind. I salute them for the job they are doing in very trying circumstances. I may be donning the rose-tinted glasses when I say the job was a lot simpler (and more fun) in the old days.

Having said that it doesn't mean it isn't true.

> 🛡️
> Border Force
>
> **John David Clarke**
>
> In recognition of your outstanding contribution to securing the border during the London 2012 Olympic and Paralympic Games.
>
> Tony Smith
> Director General
> Border Force

Something nice to end with. The London games were a huge success – and it seems a lot of it was down to yours truly!